Elliott Collinson

DEAD VERSIONS OF ME

Elliott Collinson

DEAD VERSIONS OF ME

A MEMOIR
Some Versions Didn't Survive The Telling

ELLIOTT COLLINSON

2025 DVOM
A DEAD VERSIONS CREATIVE PUBLICATION

Elliott Collinson

DEAD VERSIONS OF ME
Copyright © 2025 Version Ten Publishing
All Rights Reserved.

Published by Version Ten Publishing
under the imprint name
A Dead Versions Creative Publication

Except as permitted under the Australian Copyright Act 1968 (for example, a fair dealing for the purposes of study, research, criticism or review). No part of this book may be reproduced, stored in a retrieval system, or transmitted in any form or by any means, either electronic, mechanical, photocopying, recording, or otherwise, without the prior written permission of the publisher, except in the case of brief quotations embodied in critical articles or reviews.

This is a work of creative non-fiction. Some names, characters, events, and dialogue have been fictionalized or rearranged to protect privacy or enhance narrative clarity. The emotional truth, however, remains intact.

For permissions, media inquiries, or strange echoes from your past, contact:

Author: Elliott Collinson
Author contact: theauthor@deadversionsofme.com
Instagram: @deadversionsofme
Website: www.deadversionsofme.com

Cover & Interior Design: Elliott Collinson
Publisher: A Dead Versions Creative Publication
ISBN: 978-1-7642291-2-8 (Paperback)
978-1-7642291-0-4 (Dust Jacket Hardcover)
eBook Also Available
First Edition: 2025

Disclaimer

The material in this publication is of a general nature and does not constitute professional advice. It is not intended to provide specific guidance for particular circumstances and should not be relied upon as the basis for any decision to act or not act. Readers should seek professional support where appropriate. To the maximum extent permitted by law, the author and publisher disclaim all responsibility and liability for any loss or damage incurred by any person relying on the information in this publication.

Elliott Collinson

Dedication

To the versions of me that tried.
Some were useful.
Some were poetic.
Most were delusional.
All are now unemployed.

Best of luck in your next life.

Elliott Collinson

TABLE OF CONTENTS

Prologue:	*The Illness I Invented by Elliott Collinson*	14
Chapter 1:	*The Spark*	19
Chapter 2:	*Method Writing*	35
Chapter 3:	*Dead Versions Of Me*	48
Chapter 4:	*The High*	68
Chapter 5:	*The Reckoning*	84
Chapter 6:	*The Survivor*	92
Chapter 7:	*The Illusion of Balance*	115
Chapter 8:	*The Becoming*	130
Chapter 9:	*The Allusion Letters*	137
Part I: *The Kindness of Misunderstanding*		138
Part II: *Echoes Without Ears*		142
Part III: *The Confrontation*		146
Part IV: *The Mirror Isn't For You*		149
Part V: *The Empathy Olympics*		153
Part VI.A: *When the Past Becomes Possessive*		158
Part VI.B: *When the Past Starts Answering Back*		163
Part VII: *The Performance of Healing*		169
Part VIII: *The Illusion of Closure*		174
Part IX: *The One Who Walked Out Of The Fire*		178
Chapter X:	*Self-Inflicted Bipolar*	182

Expansion Chapters

Expansion I:	*Field Guide To The Ghosts*	191
Expansion II:	*A Letter To The Ghost Who Was Never Written*	196
Expansion III:	*The Version Who Refused To Perform*	199
Expansion IV:	*Methods Of Disappearing*	202
Expansion V:	*I Was Never The Chosen One*	206
Expansion VI:	*A Letter Left Unsent*	209
Bonus Chapter:	*Interview with the Future Self*	212
Final Chapter:	*The Listener*	218
Afterword	Acknowledgements	221
About the Author		225

Elliott Collinson

Dead Versions Of Me

First, there was fire.
Then ash, then silence,
Then a whisper that sounded like me.
This is what came after.

Elliott Collinson

PROLOGUE
The Illness I Invented

I didn't set out to make myself sick, but somewhere along the way, writing ceased to be a tool and became a symptom. I—too curious, too obsessive, too damned romantic about suffering, let it happen. I wrote until I couldn't tell what was real anymore, chasing truth through fiction as though it owed me something. I didn't want healing. I wanted catharsis. I wanted to be cracked open and remade, character by character, draft by draft. Somewhere in that ritual, I broke something that didn't grow back the same.

There's no diagnosis for what I went through, no checkbox in the DSM. If there had been, maybe I would've leaned on it as a crutch, maybe it would've helped people understand why I stopped answering calls, skipped birthdays, became a version of me they didn't recognize. But what I had wasn't a clean disorder. It was a self-designed distortion. A kind of self-inflicted bipolar, rooted not in biology, but in imagination. I didn't inherit this. I created it, fed it and built my life around it. I gave it a name and called it writing.

What started as a simple act of storytelling soon evolved into something much more consuming, and personally captivating. At first, it was just about telling stories. Simple enough. Escape when existence feels cramped, clamorous. But as I got better, sharper, more immersed in my process, the boundaries started to rot. I'd dive so deep into a character's psyche that I'd forget where mine ended. I'd map their trauma with such precision that I'd wake up grieving their losses as if they were mine. And maybe, in some way, they were. I wasn't writing fiction—I was exorcising ghosts. Ghosts wearing my face. Ghosts I didn't even know I'd buried, or perhaps ghosts I'd never known to mourn.

I created versions of myself. Hundreds, maybe thousands, each one carrying a piece of the truth I couldn't say out loud. Some were stronger than me. Some were monsters. Others were so delicate, so desperate, I could feel the weight of their fragility, like glass shattering each time I read them back. I killed most of them by the final act. Some deserved it. Some didn't. But every death left a scar. That's the part no one talks about. How storytelling can become a graveyard. How you start confusing character arcs with your own evolution. How eventually, you start to believe that pain is what makes the writing worth reading. That you must suffer beautifully for it to matter.

People told me to "take a break." As if I could walk away from the altar I built. As if it wasn't already etched into how I thought, breathed, and processed the world. I didn't write because I wanted to. I wrote because *I had to.* There was no off switch. No safe zone. Just the compulsion to dive back in. To get it right. To squeeze one more line of truth from whatever emotional limb I hadn't already amputated.

And maybe that's why I lost parts of myself along the way. Relationships. Sleep. Sanity. The ability to just "be" without narrating it in my head. I stopped experiencing moments and started *crafting* them. Watching myself cry, wondering how it would read on the page. Arguing with someone I love, only to mentally rewrite the scene minutes later, giving myself a better line, a cleaner exit. Life became first draft material—every feeling rehearsed, every silence weaponized.

But don't confuse this for martyrdom. I'm not noble for breaking myself open. I'm not proud of the damage I did chasing these stories. I've hurt people. I've ghosted people. I've become a stranger to versions of myself I once swore to protect. And for what? A few pages that felt honest? A character that said what I never had the guts to say?

Still—I keep writing.

Maybe because it's all I know. Maybe because the moment I stop, the silence starts to feel like death. Or maybe because deep down, I believe there's a version of me, ten years from now, still standing. Still writing. Scarred but sober. Someone who survived the noise long enough to give it shape. I don't know him yet. But I've seen glimpses. Sometimes I wonder if he's the one writing this now— looking back at me, disgusted and grateful all at once.

This isn't a redemption arc. I'm not promising answers. I didn't write this book to inspire you. I wrote it because I needed to survive what it took to write the others. Because there was nowhere else left to put the weight. Because if I didn't write this one… I don't think I'd be here at all.

So don't expect a clean journey. Don't expect triumph. Expect truth. And maybe—if I've done my job right— you'll see your own dead versions, too.

CHAPTER 1
THE SPARK

"He didn't survive. I did. But I still carry his funeral in my mouth."

He didn't survive because he was strong.
He survived because he got tired of dying.
There is nothing romantic about barely breathing.
This version just wanted to live.

I didn't grow up thinking I'd become a writer. Back then, when my world revolved around batting cages, I would've laughed and called it soft. Writing wasn't the plan. It wasn't even on the radar. Baseball was everything.

It wasn't a diagnosis. There was nothing to tick in a manual. If there had been, I probably would've leaned on it. Explained the missed calls. The empty chairs. But what I had wasn't clean. It was self-designed—a distortion I built, fed, and named writing.

In 2000, having just experienced a major car accident (where to this day I know a spark was tweaked in my soul) I moved from Perth to Sydney to chase that dream. I was young, cocky, and sure of who I was—or at least who I thought I needed to be. I trained hard. I played harder. And when I wasn't on the field, I threw myself into the Sydney nightlife like a man trying to fill every second of silence with noise. Clubs, parties, late nights that bled into early mornings. It felt like freedom—probably just distraction dressed as ambition. Or maybe it was just distraction dressed for ambition. I didn't really stop to ask.

But even then, beneath the surface, something quieter had begun. I started writing letters to my parents—handwritten, honest, sometimes too honest. I'd sit down in the middle of that chaos and tell them everything. How I felt. What I was chasing. What I feared. I didn't think of it as writing at the time. I thought of it as staying connected, trying to explain a version of myself they couldn't see anymore. Years later, my mum handed those letters back. They were yellowed, creased, the paper thin with handling. She told me they were beautiful. I don't know if I believed her at the time, but I never forgot it.

The next time I remember truly writing was a few years later—the kind that cracks something open in you—was during my first trip to the United States. I went alone. Just me and my dream of... well, I wasn't even sure what anymore. I was heading to a summer camp in Maine, tucked into the trees and lakes like something out of a coming-of-age movie. My mum was nervous. Understandably. I was crossing the world to a place I didn't know, with no one waiting on the other end except a vague promise of adventure.

I wrote letters from there too. Long, heartfelt ones. Descriptions of the camp, the kids, the oddness of being in a foreign place that somehow felt like it knew me better than home did. Those letters weren't just updates—they were stand-ins, proof I hadn't disappeared, even when I felt like I had.

But the real shift happened the second year I returned to Winona. I bought a laptop—one of those thick Dell bricks that weighed as much as guilt—and for some reason, I started writing poems. Not one or two, but dozens. About things I didn't know I'd been carrying. About the girl I fell in love with. About the ache of letting go of baseball—deeper than any injury. About the death of a dream I hadn't realised was dying until it was already gone.

Looking back, I think that was the real fracture point. Baseball wasn't just a sport. It was my identity. My future. My currency in the world. When my body started giving out—and when my mind followed—I didn't just lose a dream. I lost who I was. And in that void, I started writing. Not as a choice. As survival.

I didn't know how to process the loss, the grief, the confusion of returning to Australia and feeling like a stranger in my own life. I didn't know how to be vulnerable with anyone around me. So, I started writing—quietly, obsessively. I wasn't writing to be read. I was writing to exist.

Then in 2009, came Denouement, a short film I starred in and co-produced. The film garnered several awards in the U.S. It was raw, messy, cathartic. It proved that I could make meaning from pain. That maybe I didn't need to be a baseball player to matter. Maybe I could be something else.

I didn't realise it then, but that was the moment I got hooked. The moment I stopped seeing writing as an outlet and started seeing it as oxygen. I'd lost one identity, but I was beginning to carve out another. I wasn't just documenting my story—I was rewriting it.

And that's the dangerous thing about discovering writing too late. You don't come to it with discipline. You come to it with hunger. And hunger can turn into obsession really fast. Maybe the belief that I had to suffer to write wasn't craft at all—it was the part of me that refuses stillness, dressing control up as devotion.

It's strange, looking back now, how quiet that loss was. The death of a dream doesn't come with a funeral. No one sends flowers. There's no eulogy, no wake. Just silence. It's so powerful that even when we realise what's happened, the silence gets louder. One day, you wake up and realise the thing you've wrapped your identity around isn't coming back, and no one notices but you.

That was me after baseball. I was physically hurt, yeah. But more than that, I was psychologically fractured. I didn't want to talk about it. Didn't know how to. So, I drifted. I threw myself into the noise of being young and untethered. But at night, when the noise wore off and I was alone, I started reaching for that laptop.

Poems. Lyrics. Fragments of feeling that didn't belong to anyone else. They weren't good. Some of them were barely readable. But they were mine. Honest in a way I didn't know how to be in real life. That became the addiction—truth without confrontation. Writing let me confess without having to explain. And once I tasted that kind of freedom, I couldn't go back to ordinary conversation.

I remember sitting on the edge of my bunk at camp, staring into the dark woods outside my tent, and thinking:

"Is this it now? Is this who I am?"

Not the athlete. Not the golden boy. Just… someone with too many words and not enough ways to say them out loud.

I don't think I had the vocabulary back then to articulate it. But I felt it—deeply. The shift. The collapse. The quiet evolution. Writing didn't come to me like lightning. It came like erosion. Bit by bit, it hollowed out the part of me that used to dream of standing on a pitcher's mound and replaced it with something new. Something lonelier. More awake.

When I got back to Australia, everything felt muted. The girl I'd fallen for while overseas… things didn't last. We tried, for a while. But I wasn't really there anymore, at least not fully. She was talking to the old me, and I had already begun morphing into someone else. Someone quieter, watchful.

What followed were strange years. I floated for a while before I landed in acting classes—not because I wanted to be a performer, but because I needed a place to feel something again. Acting cracked me open in a way I didn't expect. For the first time since baseball, I had a stage. A new form of expression. A safe way to bleed in front of people and call it performance.

I threw myself into it. Helped grow the company that gave me that outlet. Encouraged others. Lifted them. There was power in that, too. That became part of the pattern—investing in others, pouring myself into building something, anything, just to not feel the hollowness of my own stalled identity.

Then came Los Angeles. A year that was supposed to launch me forward but instead twisted me in new directions. I wasn't immersed in acting the way I thought I'd be. What came, surprisingly, was painting. A whole new creative current. I found a rhythm in it, a silence that writing couldn't give me. I painted obsessively—raw, layered pieces full of motion and texture, imperfect, but honest, and a close friend—an artist—kept me grounded.

And yet one of the cleanest lines I've ever written arrived after an hour of quiet painting—the sentence walked in untouched, because I finally gave it silence.

I created a full body of work and for once, the expression didn't need words.

And yet, even then, I felt the pull of story. Of film. Of constructing meaning from fragments.

When I returned to Australia, I came back with a different kind of hunger. No longer trying to be in someone else's story, I wanted to make my own. That's when Denouement appeared. The opportunity to produce a short film and bring something real into the world. I wasn't the writer, but I was deeply inside the process. The vision. The execution. The pressure and the beauty of making something out of nothing.

It wasn't just a film. It was a turning point. The first time I saw that maybe I had the bones to build something that mattered. That maybe the string of artistic detours I'd taken wasn't failure—it was evolution.

And that was the spark. Not a single moment, but the slow burn of letters, losses, the poems, the heartbreak, the acting, the paint, the dark nights staring at the ceiling asking, "What the fuck am I doing with my life?" That was the real beginning. Not of a career. Of an identity.

That moment did something to me. It told me that maybe I wasn't crazy. That maybe this thing inside me—the pull toward narrative, toward emotion, toward examining the wreckage—wasn't just self-indulgence. Maybe it was a direction. It didn't fix me. But it focused me. After Denouement, something shifted.

Recognition didn't soothe me—it licensed me to go deeper.

The film did well. Better than any of us expected. It made the rounds through the festival circuit, picked up awards, stirred conversations. It was surreal, watching something you helped bring into the world gain recognition like that. I wasn't the writer—but I was part of its bones. And in that success, I felt something unfamiliar: momentum.

I didn't really celebrate. It was a great time with my fellow filmmakers, and of course I knew how, but inside I felt it—a door creaking open. One I hadn't dared to knock on before.

Then came the next opportunity. A writer friend was interested in helping me develop Denouement into the full extended film story it so deserved. At this point I was not a seasoned screenplay writer. Not even someone who understood what I should do. She asked if I'd be interested in co-writing it. I said yes before my self-doubt could talk me out of it.

It was the first time I really co-wrote something—not just scribbled into the void or wrote in bursts of private catharsis. This was structure. This was dialogue. Character. Stakes. A world built from the ground up. I dove in the only way I knew how: headfirst, no brakes. I delved so deep I think that's where the onset of my condition began.

We spent weeks, then months, and now years shaping it. Draft after draft. Rewrites that cut to the bone. Late-night phone calls for hours and arguments about character arcs and theme. And underneath it all, the pulse of something bigger.

That script wasn't just a story—it was a test. Could I do this? Not just write for me, but build something that could stand? Could hold weight? Could live outside of me? Something inside me said yes.

Maybe that's when I started thinking bigger. I learnt so much in this process about how to write screenplays with structure and eloquence. About full-length features. About trilogies. About mythologies and symbols and emotional universes that stretched beyond a single screenplay. My mind didn't want to write stories anymore. It wanted to write worlds. And in that ambition, I started losing track of where I ended and the work began.

That was the beginning of Revelations. My first true dive into the deep. The characters weren't just written—they were excavated. Each one a shadow of something I hadn't dealt with. A regret. A suppressed truth. A fractured part of myself I had buried or pretended to evolve from. I created a mythology not to entertain, but to catalogue and contain the ghosts.

Revelations wasn't just writing. It was a descent. A method of digging so far inward I started to forget where the fiction ended, and I began. That project taught me the terrifying joy of full immersion. Of becoming the character to the point it warped the way I thought, spoke, and felt in the real world.

All I knew was I was no longer someone who wanted to write. I was someone who had to. There was no hobby here. No hobbyist. The stories weren't coming from me—they were coming for me. I had no idea what it would cost. Only that I couldn't turn it off. That part didn't scare me yet.

Back then, I didn't know this was the beginning. That one day, I'd be writing entire characters just to mourn versions of myself that never got to live. I didn't know I'd create entire fictional lives just to survive my own. I didn't have a process in the beginning. Not really. Not in the structured, disciplined sense that seasoned writers talk about.

What I had was compulsion. I didn't write with an outline. I wrote like a man chasing a vision in the dark feeling along the walls, slamming into dead ends, doubling back, covered in metaphorical bruises, but unable to stop moving.

There were days I wouldn't eat until nightfall and nights that ran into sunrise. I'd sit in front of the screen and my spine ached and I forgot how to speak in full sentences. Sometimes I didn't know if what I was writing was brilliant or borderline psychotic. But I didn't care. It wasn't about quality—it was about release. There was something inside me I couldn't carry anymore unless I gave it form.

And I started needing pain to write. It was effective, and reckless—a craft choice that blurred into a sort of self-harm.

Not drama. Not inconvenience. Real, internal rupture. The kind you manufacture when you dig into your own unresolved history and rip it open just to get the line right. I'd play music that shattered me. Watch scenes that left me gutted. I'd trigger myself on purpose—just to access the state I believed my characters needed to live in. I became my own antagonist. My own method actor. My own collateral damage.

I learned it on Revelations: I looped a song that wrecked me and wrote a father-son goodbye I'd never lived, sobbing at the keyboard—but the scene finally breathed.

And that's when I started to notice something darker.

The better the writing got, the worse I became. As the characters sharpened into emotional truth, I blurred. I'd come out of writing sessions in a fog. Forget what day it was. I got lost in conversations; part of me was still stuck in a scene that hadn't finished playing out. I began writing arguments I'd never had—but they lingered like real memories. I carried grief that wasn't mine. Rage that wasn't mine. Love for people who didn't exist.

And yet... I couldn't let it go.

That's when it hit me:

The readers got the heat. The people who loved me got the ash.

I wasn't writing characters anymore. I was writing versions of me.

The storylines weren't fiction. They were eulogies.

The characters weren't inventions. They were ghosts.

Fractured, repressed, reshaped into different timelines. Every scene, every life I built, was another way to examine who I might've been. Or who I lost. Or who I never had the courage to become.

And the process?

The process was exorcism.

No one saw it happening at the time. On the outside, I was functioning. Conversations. Coffee meetings. Project plans. But inside, I was breaking in controlled bursts. The terrifying part? I liked it. I liked the collapse. I liked the proximity to something that felt undeniably real. I liked watching myself fall apart in the name of something that might outlive me.

If I'm wrong about needing pain, then I burned years I didn't have—sleep, love, trust—paying a price the work never asked me to pay.

That's what it means to write from the wound. Not the scar. Not the healing. The wound. And I hadn't even hit bottom yet.

The truth was, by that point, I wasn't looking for ideas anymore. I wasn't mapping character arcs or plotting outcomes. The characters were already alive in my head. Fully formed. Fully fledged. All wanting to speak. All wanting their say.

They weren't just characters anymore. They were voices. Ghosts. Emotional hitchhikers.

Sometimes I'd be driving down the highway and one of them would break through the static—sharp, insistent, urgent. A line of dialogue. A moment of clarity. A buried truth they were ready to confess. The ideas would flood like possession. I'd scramble for my phone, for paper, for anything to capture it before it vanished. It's a miracle I didn't crash—doing 100 km/h with one hand on the wheel, the other fumbling for voice memos.

But sometimes, I wasn't fast enough. I'd lose the thread. The scene. The line. Gone. And then, like clockwork, it would come back. The voice again, whispering:

"Why didn't you write it down when I gave it to you?"

They didn't care that I was tired. Or driving. Or trying to sleep. They didn't know what time it was. They didn't care that I was human. They just knew I was theirs. Their vessel. The messenger. The scribe.

The ideas didn't ask. They demanded. Like dreams that fade if you don't grab them by the throat. If I didn't catch them, they punished me—with silence, or repetition, or worse: forgetfulness.

This wasn't brainstorming anymore. This was channelling. And it felt sacred, dangerous and addictive.

This was only the beginning of what I would come to understand as Method Writing. I thought I was writing the stories, but soon I'd realise... they were writing me.

But the seed was already there. The fracture had formed. And in that fracture, something took root.

I wasn't just becoming a writer. I was becoming haunted— and it scared the hell out of me.

CHAPTER 2
METHOD WRITING

"The deeper you go into your characters, the more you lose track of which pain was yours to begin with."

The truth didn't break him.
It just stripped him of excuses.
What was left wasn't pretty,
but it finally made sense.

If you want to know what it means to take your passion seriously, ask yourself this:

Are you willing to lose your balance for it?

Because that's what it takes. Not half-steps. Not well-timed routines or "inspiration when it hits." Not the kind of commitment you pencil into your calendar between other things. I'm talking about the kind of devotion that eats away at your relationships. That hijacks your sleep. That makes people wonder if you're all right—because, in truth, you're probably not.

Writing—real writing—isn't a lifestyle. It's a haunting. It starts with curiosity, sure. An idea. A flicker of something. But if you do it right—if you really go in—it becomes a full-body possession. You don't live your life and write around it. You write, and everything else becomes noise you either fold into the work or push out to survive.

I didn't understand that at first. I thought I was just developing my voice. Building something artistic. But what I was really doing was building a trapdoor—one I kept falling through, each time landing deeper, darker, further from the version of me who started this.

The difference between passion and obsession is how much of yourself you're willing to lose in the process. And I was all in. No roadmap. No parachute. Just pain dressed as instinct.

There were no shortcuts. No secret hacks. The only way I got better was by bleeding for it. Digging so far into my own psychology that I couldn't tell if I was writing characters or diagnosing myself in disguise. I'd wake up thinking like them. Walk around with their shame in my chest. And the strange thing was—it worked. The more I cracked myself open, the more honest the writing became. But honesty, when weaponised, is a brutal thing. Especially when you turn it on yourself.

The first time I pushed it too far, I wrote a confession scene I'd been dodging for months. I starved the room of music, sat with a memory I'd avoided, and the dialogue arrived without decoration—exact, exhausted, undeniable.

I wrote like I was running out of time. Like if I didn't get the truth out today, it might never come again. I treated it like war. Like survival. Not because I wanted to suffer—but because I wanted to mean it. Every word. Every beat. Every page.

And then there were lines that only arrived after a walk and a glass of water. The page doesn't always want blood—sometimes it wants oxygen.

The voice didn't arrive. It interrupted. "You're late." I was on the M4, one hand on the wheel, when the words dropped like a verdict. I didn't argue. I just started writing in my head.

That's what I mean when I say, "method writing." It's not a technique. It's a toll. And the ones who don't understand that—they won't make it past page ten.

If you force it without consent, it reads like performance; if you enter it without limits, it reads like self-harm.

Most writers say they build their characters. That they sculpt them from imagination and add layers of backstory like paint on canvas. I didn't build mine. I became them. And they became me. I wrote notes, so many I can't remember nor count. Some typed, some scribbled in notebooks, scraps of paper, margins of receipts. Character histories. Timelines. Birthdays. Family trauma. Entire childhoods, sketched out just to understand how a character held a pen. Or why they drank tea instead of coffee. Or what lie they told themselves to sleep at night.

It wasn't enough to write them into a scene. I needed to know why they deserved to exist in the first place. Every job, every wound, every twitch of their personality had to come from something real. If one of them was a detective, I needed to know the process behind every courtroom they stepped into. The legal system. Chain of custody. Forensic protocols. Interview rhythms. I researched things I had no business knowing—because the story demanded it. Because they demanded it.

The characters spoke through me. That's not metaphor. That's how it felt. I didn't create their tone—I heard it. I didn't assign them pasts—I watched them unfold. Their pain wasn't mine. I carried it anyway. And in time, I realised I was no longer crafting them. I was channelling them.

Each one began to infiltrate my real life.

Some taught me how to carry rage and keep it hidden beneath precision. Some taught me discipline, control, restraint. Some taught me how to break people with a sentence and regret it instantly. They weren't just figments. They became emotional systems I lived inside of. And they started to shape the way I saw the world.

They altered how I drove. How I walked. How I scanned a room. They reprogrammed my instincts. And the deeper I went, the harder it was to pull out.

Some nights I wrote letters to future versions of myself—letters I would later call Dead Versions of Me. I didn't know why yet, only that I needed to document what was happening. Proof that I was still alive, even as the characters I was writing consumed me.

There were nights I started writing at 10pm. It would take me an hour to get into the boat—into the mindset—and then I'd drift into the current. Taken by something I didn't control. I'd blink, and it would be 6am. The sun coming up. Time to shower, change, and go to work. No sleep. No break. But I didn't care. Because in that flow state, the rules of the real world didn't matter. Those hours didn't feel like hours. They felt like thirty minutes in another universe.

I sacrificed everything for those nights. Time. Energy. Rest. Relationships. Sanity. Sometimes even self-respect.

But I did it because I believed—and still believe—that to honour a story, you must suffer for it. You must live inside it long enough to let it scar you. You must become so intimate with your creation that it leaves a mark on your body, your voice, your thoughts.

Anything less is performance. What I was doing wasn't performance. It was possession. And I still wasn't done falling.

I still remember the letters. I called them Dead Versions of Me. They were written to a future self I hoped existed, letters that weren't encouragement, but warnings. Every single one a fractured autobiography of someone I used to be, someone I abandoned, someone I buried along the way. A graveyard of selves I had to write my way through, just to stay alive long enough to become something better.

I wrote things like:

The letters didn't comfort me; they conscripted me.

"Dear future self, I'm writing from the wreckage of a past life I couldn't save. I've buried so many versions of myself just to make it here. And still... I don't know if I'm enough. But you—you need to believe again. Because you're all we've got left."

And others that read:

"Some version of me didn't make it. This is the one that did. Protect him. Finish what he started."

Those letters weren't just reflective—they were confrontational. A daily reckoning. A way to remind myself of the stakes involved. They were a promise not to repeat old patterns. A refusal to become just another name on the headstone of potential. They kept me awake at night, whispering their warnings long after I had written them.

There was one I kept coming back to—a line scrawled urgently, almost illegible:

"Your time is running out. You can't keep living life for other people. You can't keep betraying the voice inside you. Stand up. Stop lying. Start moving."

But I did lie, sometimes. Lied to myself about how far I'd come. Lied about how strong I was, how committed I felt. There were days when I woke up more ghost than human, haunted by those words. Haunted by every dead version I had let down. Haunted by how close I was to becoming just another letter in the pile.

That's why I fought so hard. Why I bled into every page. Because I wasn't writing for an audience anymore—I was writing to avoid my own funeral. To quiet the voices long enough to hear my own again.

Method Writing wasn't about performance. It wasn't even about art. It was about survival. It was about proving, even if only to myself, that I could keep a promise made to the dead because if I didn't—if I stopped—those letters would stop being warnings. They'd become prophecy. And I wasn't ready for my story to end like that.

Personal Consequences

Devotion reads like betrayal to the people who care.

There were moments when friends stopped calling. Invitations went unanswered. Loved ones would text, "Hey, are you okay? You've gone quiet." I'd answer with a vague "Busy," but the truth was simpler and harder—I was living inside someone else's life, and my own felt like a stranger. Birthdays, casual dinners, anniversaries slipped by while I sat hunched over a keyboard and mugs of half cold coffee. The guilt piled up—yet I told myself, they can't understand. In the silence, I felt both liberated and utterly isolated.

Conversations derailed because my mind was somewhere else—reworking dialogue, carrying a character's grief into a casual exchange. Apologies blurred into habit. Some people drifted away; a few stayed, wary and worried. Devotion to craft can feel like betrayal to those who care.

Physical & Mental Toll

My body staged quiet mutiny. Chronic fatigue wrapped

itself around my spine. Anxiety spiked whenever a character's crisis felt too real. Sleep became a battleground: dreams invaded by unfinished scenes or nights where rest never came because my mind refused to shut down until the next page existed. I hovered between hyperfocus and collapse—emotionally numb yet haunted.

Rituals & Obsessions

Immersion demanded ritual. A playlist looping the exact mood of a scene. Incense curling through half-darkness. A wall of index cards—dialogue scraps, thematic symbols, faces torn from magazines. Controlled chaos. Sometimes I wore a character's jacket, sipped their tea, walked the city streets in their cadence. Even mundane errands turned into reconnaissance: a clerk's bored tone, the fluorescent hush of a hospital corridor, the echo of a stairwell—everything was story fodder.

Blurring Reality

Occasionally I caught a glimpse of myself in a window—and it wasn't me staring back. Friends noticed new cadences, borrowed phrases. Once, I scolded a colleague in a voice I'd written for someone else and felt the jolt of a boundary snapping. In public I mumbled dialogue, in private I argued with ghosts. Dreams became alternate drafts; I woke unsure whether a memory belonged to life or fiction; the blue hum of the fridge at 3 a.m. was sometimes the only proof I was still in the room.

Insight from the Edge

Amid the chaos came flashes of clarity. Immersion revealed hidden rooms of the psyche—truths I'd never confront without fiction's mask. Empathy deepened; perspective widened. Yet I also saw the danger: devotion turning self-destructive. Some nights I wondered if the scars left by writing were worth the words gained.

A hard epiphany surfaced: the stories didn't just serve the characters—they served me. They held a mirror to wounds and desires long buried. Method Writing sharpened my craft, but it also sliced into the core of who I thought I was.

The Future Watching Me

Somewhere in the haze of all that effort—bloodshot eyes, cramped hands, spine curved like a broken bridge over the keyboard—I swear I caught his attention.

The version of me twenty-five years ahead—the one who made it, the one I was writing letters to while I was buried in *Revelations*. He's ten years older now, closer, as if the distance between us has started to collapse. For a moment, I believed he was watching, and that these sleepless nights could be the hinge on which everything turned.

He watched from a vantage point I can't fathom, and for a brief moment, terrifying and glorious, he believed I might finally be the one who wouldn't quit. The version who would finish what none of the others ever managed.

And then... I didn't.

I let the doubts in. Let excuses grow louder than vision. I did the work, but I pulled back just enough to break momentum, just enough to let the timid version of me climb into the driver's seat.

I know what that future-self did when he saw it happen. He crossed me out. Filed me under Almost. Another dead leaf in the archive of potential. That's the cruellest part: knowing I had him believing and then gave him every reason not to.

Crossroads

Eventually I understood this approach couldn't last forever. There had to be distance—moments to step out of the current and breathe. Yet I knew I would always return;

once you've tasted that intimacy with creation, ordinary life feels thin.

By the end of this phase I stood at a crossroads: plunge deeper into the abyss or learn to integrate the method without self-destructing. The choice would shape everything that followed and that is where the next chapter begins. Depth was easy. Integration would demand a different kind of courage.

CHAPTER 3
DEAD VERSIONS OF ME

"Every version of yourself you outlive becomes another ghost you have to carry. Kill enough of them, and eventually you forget which one was ever real."

Some ghosts don't haunt you.
They wait patiently in old mirrors,
just to see if you'll lie to them again.
He used to.

It started quietly.

At first, the writing was enough. Characters spoke. Stories unfolded. The process consumed me. Then the noise shifted. It wasn't characters anymore. It was the versions of me—the ones I thought I'd buried.

Dead Versions Of Me

They didn't knock. They just arrived.

Like ghosts returning to a house I never realised I still owned.

I thought writing was about creation. But as the months dragged on, I realised I was writing more funerals than births. Each story I told was built on the back of a version of myself that didn't survive. The optimist. The golden boy. The romantic. The hopeful athlete. The one who thought dreams were linear.

They were gone.

And I had killed them.

Not out of malice, but out of necessity.

The deeper I wrote, the more vivid they became. I could see their faces. Versions of myself frozen at different stages, as if waiting for me to acknowledge them. Some I pitied. Some I resented. Some I mourned without knowing why.

I couldn't shake them.

One night, unable to sleep, I opened a blank document. My hands hovered above the keys, shaking slightly. My heartbeat faster than it should have. I didn't know what I was doing. But my fingers started moving before my mind caught up.

"You never risked it," I typed. "You told yourself you were protecting stability. Protecting your family. Your peace." I paused. My breath caught. I hit backspace. Rewrote it. "But I know what you were protecting—your fear." It wasn't fiction. It was a confession.

I stared at the words. The version I was speaking to hovered behind my shoulder—the one who never left Perth, who stayed safe, who let caution kill his potential long before anything else did.

He was the first. But not the last. The next night, I opened the file again. A different face came forward.

"You held onto the game like it owed you something."

The version who clung to baseball long after his body gave out. The one who couldn't accept the injury. The fracture. The death of a dream that had once defined everything.

"You let your pride rot into resentment," I wrote, fingers trembling. "I almost became you."

I leaned back. Closed my eyes. Saw another face waiting. The one who almost stayed with the girl. The version who traded purpose for comfort. Who could have lived a quiet, easy life. Safe. Predictable. Stagnant.

"You almost convinced me," I whispered as I typed, "that love could replace purpose. That routine could replace meaning. I envied you sometimes. I hated you more. You were the most dangerous of them all—because you almost made me settle."

The words poured like confessions at a wake. I wasn't writing to purge them. I was documenting them. The graveyard inside me grew. Every risk I took. Every sacrifice I made. Every version I outlived. They lined up like silent witnesses behind me.

And as I stared into that growing archive, I found myself asking the question I wasn't ready to face:

How many more of me would I have to kill just to become the version that finally survives?

I told myself I was in control. That writing these letters gave me power over them. That naming them meant I was free of them. But that was the first lie. They didn't leave. They lingered. Sometimes I'd see them out of the corner of my eye, like faint reflections in glass. Not ghosts. Not hallucinations. Just... echoes. Standing just far enough behind me that I couldn't turn and face them directly.

The safe one. The bitter one. The one who almost stayed. The one who almost burned it all down.

And the worst one—the one I hadn't written yet. The one I was becoming.

The weight of them sat on my chest in the quiet hours. It wasn't fear of failure that haunted me. It was something heavier—something colder. The fear of adding one more to the pile.

Every time I sat at that desk, I knew the stakes. Finish this chapter or die another version. Push deeper or get crossed off like the others. The graveyard didn't care how hard I worked—it only cared about outcomes. It counted survivors.

There were nights I'd whisper to myself before I started writing:

"Don't become another letter."

Some days I wondered how many versions of me already existed in that archive. How many silent selves I'd buried without even noticing. The ones I didn't mourn. The ones who died quietly in small acts of compromise. The ones who gave up a little at a time until there was nothing left to save. I kept writing anyway because the alternative was worse.

The Descent Deepens

There's something few people tell you about chasing your passion with everything you have.

They talk about sacrifice. They talk about obsession. But they never talk about the quiet extinction of self that happens along the way. I was no longer afraid of failure. I was afraid of becoming empty. Because once you burn through enough versions of yourself, you start wondering what's left. What happens when the last one dies? When the final version you're fighting to become collapses under the same weight that killed the others?

Would there even be a "me" left? Or just pages. Just words. Just echoes of someone who almost made it. That thought haunted me more than any failure ever could.

And yet one of the cleanest lines came after a long walk and water. The page doesn't always want blood—sometimes it wants oxygen.

There were moments—late nights, heavy-eyed, wired on caffeine and desperation—where I'd stare at the blinking cursor and whisper to no one:

I learned it again on an interrogation scene I'd been dodging for months: I starved the room of music, sat with a memory I'd avoided, and the dialogue arrived without decoration—exact, exhausted, undeniable.

"Don't let this be the last version." The writing no longer felt like progress; it felt like survival. Each scene was a small victory against extinction. Another breath. But the price kept rising. With every word that lived on the page, something inside me dimmed. I could feel the ledger being balanced.

The world outside started slipping through my fingers.

I'd sit at dinner with friends and hear characters speaking through me. My tone shifted, my language borrowed. Someone would pause mid-conversation and glance at me like I'd said something sharp, something unfamiliar. And I wouldn't even realise it.

Sometimes I'd catch myself mid-thought, rehearsing dialogue while someone else was talking, barely hearing them at all. I wasn't present. Not fully. The scenes in my mind were louder than the voices around me.

There were mornings I'd show up to work hollowed out, still carrying the residue of whatever life I'd been inhabiting the night before. My colleagues thought I was distracted. Or tired. Or lost in my own head. They were right. But they had no idea how deep it went. They didn't see the graveyard I carried. They didn't hear the versions whispering.

The Dying Versions

It didn't always happen when I was writing. Sometimes it struck randomly. Driving. Showering. Sitting in meetings. A sudden, cold pull from somewhere inside. Like one of them had decided it was time.

Another version dying.

Another silent exit.

I could almost feel them slipping—like something pulling apart behind my chest. A weight lifting off my body. Not relief, exactly. More like emptiness expanding. The pain would crest suddenly. It was intense and sharp, like a mental scream I couldn't translate into words, and then it would drop. Numbness would take its place.

A hollow quiet.

It reminded me of that sensation people describe after taking strong pain medication. The unbearable tension peaks...and then simply let's go. The brain gives up. The signal gets silenced.

Only I wasn't medicated. It was my mind shutting doors. Closing files. Deleting lives. And every time it happened, I knew exactly what I was feeling: Another version of me had just died. They didn't always go quietly. Sometimes I felt their cries—silent screams clawing at the edge of my consciousness. Wait. Don't erase me. I'm still here.

But the work required sacrifices. And the longer I stayed in this process, the more I understood: This was the price of choosing oneself. One version that might survive. All the others had to go.

I became strangely accustomed to it. The quiet loss. The odd calm that followed.

It was like living with an invisible kill switch—never knowing which part of me would vanish next.

The Root Memory

This didn't start with writing. I've always known that. It started long before.

When I was six—maybe seven—it began. The nightmares weren't just bad dreams. They were something else entirely. Violent. Violent in a way a child shouldn't be able to describe. My parents called them night terrors, but even they knew it wasn't that simple.

I would go to bed like any other kid. Tired. Normal. And then sometime in the middle of the night, it would take me. I never saw it coming. The pressure would build inside my chest as I slept, like something pressing down from the ceiling above me. Like I was being pinned before I was even fully asleep. My breathing would change. The air would feel heavier, thicker.

And then he would arrive. Always him.

He wasn't a monster. He didn't crawl or growl or snarl. He was a man. Always standing in the same place inside the dream. Motionless. Watching. Waiting. His face was stern, expressionless, but his eyes never left me. Cold, almost surgical. European. Military. I didn't know what country, but I knew he didn't belong to this world. Or maybe I didn't.

I would scream. Not in the dream. In real life.

I've heard the stories told back to me over the years by my father, my brother. They heard my screams first—the sharp, broken, blood-curdling kind that makes your stomach flip before you even reach the bedroom. My father would burst in, my brother behind him, both trying to wake me, shaking my body, calling my name. But I was somewhere else. My eyes would be open, but I wasn't awake.

And that's when it got worse. It wasn't just the screaming. I spoke. But not in English. Not even in broken nonsense. Full sentences. Full commands. Words pouring out of me in a language I didn't know. I don't remember the words themselves. But my father does. He remembers the tone of my voice. Different. Hardened. Cold. Like I was giving orders. Like I was someone else entirely.

No one could wake me. They tried everything—yelling, shaking me, sometimes even slapping my face gently to break the trance. Nothing worked. I would continue speaking, my body locked stiff, my mouth moving with perfect fluency in a language none of us understood.

And then it would stop.

Sometimes suddenly, like a snapped cord. Sometimes slowly, my body relaxing as if it were releasing the thing that had taken over. I'd be drenched in sweat, my chest rising and falling like I'd just run for miles. My father would hold me afterwards, but even he admitted later that in those moments, he wasn't sure who he was holding.

And then, years later, I met someone who felt like him. He became like a brother.

The dreams faded over time. I learned to bury them. To push them down beneath layers of growing up, of distractions, of normal life. But the fear never really left. It stayed, dormant. Waiting. Like he was still watching.

And then, years later, I really feel as though I met him. Became like a brother.

I don't know what to call it. Connection. Pattern. Inheritance. But it felt older than me—like it had been shaping my life long before I had words for it.

What if the versions I've been killing weren't born on the page? What if they've been following me across lives—if not literally, then psychologically—dying and resurfacing, pressing me toward something I still don't understand?

I believe we're not here by accident; some souls stay connected. We carry each other forward. Sometimes as reminders. Sometimes as warnings. The writing. The voices. The graveyard of dead versions inside me. It was never just the work. It was never just my process. It had been there all along.

The versions I've been killing weren't born on the page. They've been following me through every life I've lived. Dying and resurfacing. Dying and resurfacing. Each one pushing me toward something I still didn't fully understand. What I know is there is a connection with these versions of me that I am killing off and the versions of me I used to be in past lives. Was I doing a self-cleanse of my soul?

Even in life, there's death.

And even after death, there's still something waiting.

If that's true—if the weight predates the work—then writing wasn't the origin. It was the instrument.

The Purge

For years I had believed the writing was about telling stories. About creating. About becoming someone new. But as I stared at the growing collection of characters and voices in my head—the versions of myself I was building and burying—a new thought started gnawing at me.

What if I wasn't creating them at all? What if they were already there?

What if I'd carried these versions with me through every life I've lived, dragging their shadows behind me, one lifetime after another?

And what if the writing wasn't therapy? What if it was execution?

I started to see the pattern. The compulsion. The need. Each time I went deeper into a story, I wasn't just developing a character—I was dissecting a part of myself. Cutting into the tissue of old identities that no longer served me. Versions that clung too tightly to comfort, to ego, to failure. Versions that, if left unchecked, would rise again.

I wasn't just writing. I was performing a kind of self-exorcism. Every scene I completed felt like another body quietly being hauled off the stage. Another version neutralized and silenced. Removed from circulation. There was something cold about it. Mechanical. Like a serial killer working through a list.

The first kills were easy. The obvious ones. The version who stayed safe. The version who clung to failure. The version who almost surrendered everything for comfort. But the more I wrote, the harder it became. The more complex the versions were. The ones I nearly became. The ones who looked too much like me right now.

And every time I finished purging one, I felt lighter. Clearer. Like the painkillers had kicked in again. That sharp edge of tension dissolving into numb silence.

But there was always another. Always one more version waiting behind the next story, behind the next script, behind the next idea. Watching. Waiting to see if I would allow him to live or force him into the ground.

The most terrifying thought was the one that kept me awake long after the words had stopped coming.

What happens when I run out?

What happens when there are no more versions left to kill?

Because even then, I wasn't sure which version of me would still be standing.

The Self in Question

The further I went, the harder it became to trust myself.

For years I had believed that this version of me—the one at the keyboard, the one bleeding into these pages—was the real one. The survivor. The final product of everything that came before.

But late at night, when the house was silent and the screen glowed like an interrogation lamp in front of me, I started hearing the question whisper through the cracks:

What if you're just another one?

What if I was simply the latest version playing out his part before the next would arrive and erase me? What if I was no different than the versions I had already buried?

That was the real horror. Not the ones I had killed. But the possibility that I was never the one doing the killing. Maybe the purge was happening to me. Maybe it had always been happening. Maybe I was simply the version tasked with finishing off those who came before—but not the one who would ultimately survive.

The thought wrapped itself around my brain like a noose. It crept into everything—conversations, relationships, dreams. Sometimes I would sit across from people I loved, speaking, smiling, laughing—yet underneath it all, a voice inside me would whisper:

"They're not talking to you. They're talking to a version of you that won't exist for long."

It wasn't depression. It wasn't fear of failure. It was a creeping sense of impermanence. Of being temporary.

I began writing with an urgency I couldn't explain to anyone. Like I was racing myself. Racing time. As if the next version was already waiting in the shadows, sharpening his tools, preparing to take my place. And somewhere behind all of it, I could still feel him. The man from my childhood dreams. Watching. Silent. I didn't know if he was my guide or my executioner. All I knew was that he was always there. And that the purging wasn't finished.

Not yet.

I started to realise that what I was doing wasn't driven by choice. Not entirely. It was something closer to compulsion. A program running underneath my consciousness. A cycle I'd been locked into long before I understood what writing even was.

Each version of me that died didn't die easily. Some fought. Some begged. Some whispered long after they were gone. There were nights I could still feel their voices brushing against my skin like cold breath:

"Don't erase me."

"I was real once."

"You only exist because I failed."

And I'd sit there, alone in front of the screen, my hands trembling over the keys, knowing that I couldn't save them. Knowing that I wasn't supposed to.

The stories had to be written. The versions had to be buried. That was the agreement. The contract I never remembered signing. There was something brutally mechanical in it, but also something terrifyingly clean. Like a cosmic ledger being balanced—souls traded, identities processed, weight adjusted—until only one version remained that was finally light enough to rise. But I no longer trusted that version would be me.

I couldn't shake the feeling that I was only one iteration in a much longer sequence—a long, brutal line of souls who believed they were the one, only to be stripped down like the rest.

Maybe that's why the work always felt so violent and so desperate because some part of me knew this was my shot and some other part of me suspected I had already failed.

I would stare into the mirror some mornings—after sleepless nights, after endless hours of dissecting characters, of killing versions—and I wouldn't fully recognize the face looking back.

Was I still me or just another actor playing the role until my replacement arrived?

The purging never stopped. The writing never stopped. The dying never stopped. And beneath it all, the most horrifying question of all whispered constantly through my mind:

What if there is no final version? What if there's only the killing?

I don't know how long I stayed in that place. Days blurred into nights. Nights into something else entirely. The writing continued, but it no longer felt like creation. It felt like maintenance. Like clearing debris from some ancient battlefield. By now, the graveyard inside me was full. The versions lay still. Quiet. But not gone.

And in the silence that followed, something even more unsettling settled over me. Not fear. Not grief. Emptiness.

The work was still there. The writing still demanded my attention. But without the war raging inside me, I wasn't sure who was left to do it. The purge had stripped everything down to something hollow. Something quiet.

I told myself this was progress. That this was what I wanted and that I had cleared the path for whatever version of me was meant to remain. But even then, beneath the surface of that fragile calm, a new question had started to form—one I hadn't dared to ask until now:

Elliott Collinson

What happens to a man who has killed every version of himself but doesn't know who's left?

CHAPTER 4
THE HIGH

"You've beaten it. You're clean now. Look how sharp you are. Look at how powerful you've become."

He called it healing,
but mostly it was hiding.
The difference is subtle.
The result is not.

That's what I told myself. That's the lie the brain offers you after the purge. Not in words exactly but in sensation. The lightness. The clarity. The sudden precision like you've finally stepped out of the storm and can see the entire battlefield for the first time.

For the first time in years, I felt unburdened. The versions were gone. Their voices silenced. The graveyard was still. I moved differently. Spoke differently.

My mind felt sharper than it ever had. The writing poured out of me with ruthless efficiency. Not like before, when I had to fight for every sentence, claw through emotional wreckage to reach the truth. Now, it came clean. Swift. Like cutting through silk.

And I convinced myself that this was what mastery looked like.

Friends noticed. "You're in such a good place," they'd say. "You seem lighter. Focused."

I nodded. Smiled. Agreed. Because I wanted it to be true. Because after so many years of inner violence, I needed it to be true.

But underneath it all, I knew something had shifted. The urgency was gone. The need to feel had been replaced by the desire to control. I wasn't inside the stories anymore—I was hovering above them, pulling strings, watching lives unravel from a safe distance. Detached. Almost clinical.

And for a while, it felt good.

That's what scared me the most.

I started treating real life the same way I treated the work.

Conversations became scenes. Arguments became dialogue drills. Relationships became character studies.

I caught myself observing people mid-conversation, cataloguing their movements, their word choices, their emotional tells—as if they were actors on a set I controlled. I wasn't living moments anymore. I was documenting them, dissecting them, rewriting them in my head while they were still unfolding.

I started to enjoy the feeling. Not connection. Control. Emotions became mechanics. Pain became data.

Even with the people closest to me, I could feel it happening. Someone would open up to me sharing something raw, vulnerable —and instead of fully being there, I'd analyse it. What's their subtext? What's their wound? How would my character handle this scene differently? I was pulling threads while they were still speaking.

They noticed it too.

"*You seem distant lately,*" one friend said. "*You're here, but you're not here.*" I smiled, reassured them. But inside, I wasn't worried. I was working. That's how I justified it.

The deeper I went into this state, the more I convinced myself I had ascended into something more evolved—

beyond the fragile emotions that used to drown me. The purge had made me pure.

But in quiet moments, when no one was watching, the cracks whispered louder.

Because what I had mistaken for clarity… was numbness.

The purge didn't make me stronger. It made me hollow. And hollowness, I was beginning to realise, can be intoxicating.

Even then, a child's laugh on a train once cut straight through it—proof that feeling still had access if I let it.

I was wedged into the 8:13 to Central, head full of revisions, faces tilting past like props on a conveyor.

A toddler in a puffer jacket broke free of his mother's grip, tottered down the aisle, and landed against my shin.

He looked up—brown eyes, milk teeth—and laughed like the carriage was a playground.

The sound was unedited, raw, the opposite of everything I'd been chasing.

For a half-second the script in my head went blank.

I felt the metal pole under my palm, the oil of fingerprints, the stale breath of the heater.

My own heart thumped once—loud, unscored—and I realised I was standing in a body, not a draft.

Then the train lurched, the boy was scooped away, and the scene in my skull resumed—but the page had lost a little of its power.

It wasn't hallucination. I wasn't seeing things that weren't there. Everything around me was exactly as it should be. That was what made it worse. I was present. Physically. But it was like standing behind a pane of glass.

I watched my own life unfold, my own conversations playing out, but I wasn't inside them. The words came out of my mouth, but they didn't feel like mine. The emotions were appropriate, the tone was right, the gestures convincing — but all of it felt performed. Like a script I knew too well. Like I was playing a role I had rehearsed for years. And somewhere, just behind my own eyes, I was observing myself perform it.

Dissociation.
That's the word for it.

I didn't call it that at the time. I didn't call it anything. I told myself I was focused. Efficient. Detached in the way artists sometimes need to be. But inside, I knew something had shifted. The purge hadn't just stripped away the weaker versions. It had stripped away something essential.

Connection.

I started noticing how people looked at me differently. Longer pauses after my answers. Little frowns when I didn't laugh at the right moment. That subtle discomfort you feel around someone who seems present, but somehow... missing.

"*Are you okay?*" people would ask. I'd nod. Smile. Reassure them.
"*Never better.*"

And in many ways, I believed it. Because in this state — this numb clarity — I felt untouchable. No longer at the mercy of emotional storms. No longer ruled by the chaos that used to drive me.

But in the quiet spaces, when I was alone, I could feel it:

The weight of something missing. The distance growing between me and the world.

It was like walking through life underwater. Everything slowed. Muted. Detached but strangely beautiful. Like floating.

I knew it couldn't last. I knew I was borrowing time. But while I was inside it, The High felt clean. Cleaner than anything I had ever known.

And that's why it was so dangerous.

But even in that clarity, there were nights I needed help keeping the silence intact.

The numbness didn't always hold. Sometimes the versions whispered through the cracks. Sometimes the weight of everything I'd buried clawed at my ribs when the room was too quiet.

So I found ways to steady myself. I won't name them. Not here. The specifics don't matter. It wasn't about pleasure. It wasn't about escape. It was about control. A way to press the mute button when the voices got too close. A way to dull the sharp edges without fully breaking the illusion of mastery I had built. Just enough to take the sting off. Just enough to let me keep writing.

No one noticed. At least, not at first. Because I was functioning. I was productive. The work was getting done. And as long as the work was getting done, I could convince myself that everything else was under control. But addiction doesn't announce itself with collapse. It slips in quietly. It whispers the same lie the purge did:

"Look how sharp you are. Look how powerful you've become."

And for a while, I believed it.

The first real confrontation came sooner than I expected.

It wasn't explosive. It wasn't dramatic. It was worse than that. It was quiet.

We were sitting across from each other. A close friend. Someone who knew me before all of this. Before the obsession, before the purge, before the writing turned into survival.

They didn't start with an accusation. They started with a question.

"Are you still in there?"

The way they said it made my chest tighten.

"What do you mean?" I asked, keeping my voice light.

They looked at me for a long time before answering. "You talk differently now. You listen, but you're not really listening. Everything feels... calculated. Like you're watching all of us from behind a screen."

I forced a smile. Reassured them. "I've just been working a lot. It's nothing."

But they didn't drop it.

"No. It's not nothing."

"You're functioning, yeah. You're producing. But there's something gone. It's like you're... performing life, not living it."

I could feel my pulse climbing. I wanted to defend myself. I wanted to explain that this was just what it took. That passion demanded sacrifice. That obsession was the price of mastery. But none of those words came out. Because for the first time, I didn't fully believe them.

They leaned in, voice softer now. "I don't know if you see it yet. But whatever you've been purging, whatever you think you've gotten rid of… I think you might've cut out more than you meant to."

I laughed it off. Made a joke and changed the subject. And yet, as I walked away from that conversation, something heavy followed me. Because for the first time since the purge, I felt it:

Doubt.

A thin crack at the base of the high. And I knew once that crack spread, I wouldn't be able to stop it.

After that conversation, something shifted. Small at first. But undeniable. The silence inside me started to fracture. It came at night, mostly, when the house was still, when the work was finished, when the performance was over. The versions I thought I had buried so perfectly began pressing against the glass again. Not fully formed. Not speaking. Just… present.

I could feel them like cold weight in the room. A pressure behind my eyes. A pulse in my chest. That crawling sensation you get when you know someone's watching you from the corner of a dark room, but you're too afraid to turn your head.

They weren't gone. I had silenced them, but I hadn't killed them. And now they wanted back in. The first full rupture came without warning.

I was writing simple scenes with clean dialogue. Nothing difficult.

My breathing changed. A wave of heat rolled through my body, followed instantly by a cold sweat. It felt like I couldn't move. My heart hammered in my ears as every dead version I had written. Every face, every voice surged forward all at once. Not as characters. As selves.

The safe one.
The bitter one.
The broken one.
The one who almost ended everything.
The child who screamed in languages no one understood.

They weren't asking for resurrection. They were accusing.

"You needed us to get here," they whispered. "You stood on our bodies to survive." "And now you pretend we were never real."

I gripped the desk, trying to steady myself, but it was like holding onto a cliff edge as the wind ripped my fingers loose.

I wasn't breaking down — I was being invaded. The purge had never been permanent. It was a delay. A postponement.

And now they were returning.

I stumbled to the bathroom. Splashed water on my face. Stared into the mirror. I waited for the face I knew, the version I trusted to peek his head out and wink at me saying "keep going, we almost have it".

But what stared back felt foreign. Thin. Reconstructed. Empty in all the wrong places. Overbuilt in others. The hollow efficiency I had mistaken for strength was dissolving. The high was breaking. And in that moment, I understood something brutal:

You can only kill yourself so many times before you run out of versions.

And I was close.

The terrifying part was that it didn't just happen when I was writing. It followed me everywhere. Auditions. Work. Simple conversations. Standing in a supermarket line. Sitting in my car at a red light. That same creeping heat.

The tightness in my throat. The feeling like something behind my ribs was pushing forward — like a second heartbeat pounding inside my chest.

At times, my voice would catch mid-sentence. A slight stutter. Not from nerves. But from something deeper. It felt like I was lying—even when I wasn't. Like the act of speaking itself was betrayal. Betraying the versions that still lived inside me, screaming for acknowledgement. Betraying myself for pretending I was whole.

I could feel it in my skin sometimes — a crawling static under the surface. Like my body was rejecting its own existence. No amount of reassurance could hold it back anymore. The walls I had built during The High were too thin. And now everything I had purged was flooding back through the cracks. The numbness was collapsing under its own weight. And in its place came something much worse:

Chaos.

It didn't come as one clean breakdown. It came in waves. Sudden flashes of dissociation so intense I didn't know if I was speaking or thinking. Panic attacks that felt like my lungs were folding inward. That hollow echo in my chest when someone asked, "Are you okay?" and I couldn't even form the lie anymore.

It became harder to recognize the difference between living and observing. Between functioning and performing. Between surviving and dying. The graveyard inside me was no longer silent. The versions I thought I had executed were clawing at the dirt. They were coming back. And this time, I didn't know if I had the strength to fight them again.

If anyone had been watching closely enough, they might've called it something else. They would've given it a name. A category. A diagnosis.

"You're showing signs of dissociation." "Maybe it's unprocessed trauma." "Could be undiagnosed ADHD." "Maybe even bipolar tendencies." "There are medications that could help." I knew exactly how I must have looked.

The late nights. The obsessive focus. The impossible swings between intensity and emptiness. The flashes of clarity followed by complete collapse. Any psychiatrist would've had a file thick with labels by now.

But none of those labels fit. Not really. Because what was happening to me wasn't a chemical imbalance. It wasn't simply the mind fraying under pressure. It was something older. Something deeper. I wasn't just unravelling. I was purging. Dying and rebuilding, repeatedly. And somewhere inside me, I knew:

This wasn't a disorder. This was my design.

The last collapse came without ceremony. There was no breakdown scene. No cinematic moment of falling to my knees. Just a quiet, suffocating implosion that arrived like a hand tightening around my throat in the dark.

I sat there—alone, again—staring at the blinking cursor, unable to type a single word. My hands trembled. My chest burned. But the worst part was the silence. Not peace. Not calm. Emptiness. Not the clean emptiness I had mistaken for clarity. Not The High. This was something worse. The vacuum.

The absolute absence of self. The horrifying realization that there was nothing left to purge. No more versions to kill. No more ghosts to silence. Only me. And I wasn't enough. For years, I had believed that the sacrifice was making me stronger. That the obsession was purifying me. That the purge was necessary. But now, sitting in the aftermath, I finally saw it for what it was:

The High wasn't my victory. It was my most dangerous version yet. And it had finished its job. It left me hollowed out. Unrecognizable and efficiently destroyed. And as the weight of that final truth landed in my chest, I whispered words I never thought I'd hear myself say:

"I don't know who I am anymore."

Elliott Collinson

The purge was over. The reckoning was coming.

CHAPTER 5
THE RECKONING

"The collapse that can no longer be hidden; louder than your smile, sharp enough for even the ghosts to whisper."

> He became a different man for everyone,
> and no one ever noticed he was missing.
> He forgot how his own voice sounded,
> so he learned to write instead.

The first thing to break wasn't me. It was them. The people around me. They had been patient for years. They excused the late nights, the distant stares, the missed birthdays, the half-hearted conversations. They bought into the lie I sold so well—that this was passion, that this was sacrifice, that this was 'what it takes'. But even the most loyal have limits.

The confrontations grew sharper.

"You need to stop."
"This isn't normal anymore."
"You're not yourself."

I tried to answer but every explanation felt hollow, rehearsed. Just another script I'd memorized too well. The words came out, but my face didn't match them. They could see it. They could feel it. The distance I once controlled so easily was now showing itself in ways I couldn't hide. I still believed I could manage it. That I could hold everything together if I just kept writing. If I just stayed ahead of the collapse. But that's the lie obsession tells you right before it eats you whole.

The writing slowed.
The focus slipped.
The sharpness I had once called The High dulled into a thick, heavy fog.

I was still functioning, but it was mechanical now. It was like watching my own body operate from behind thick glass. Some days I didn't recognise my own voice. I heard myself speaking to friends, to colleagues, to strangers, and every word sounded false. Not because I was lying. But because I no longer knew which version of me was speaking.

The dissociation turned violent. Panic attacks came in waves. Moments where my chest would seize up like my heart was trying to eject itself from my body. Every time I breathed in, my chest felt tight. A sort of restrictive tourniquet around my lungs. There were nights I would stand in front of the bathroom mirror, gripping the sink, staring into my own reflection, whispering to the empty face staring back:

"Stay. Just stay."

But I could feel it slipping.

One afternoon I rested, and clarity flooded in for ten minutes—proof the fog was self-inflicted.

The problem with killing versions of yourself is they don't stay dead.

It started as flashes. Tiny, sharp jolts in the middle of otherwise normal moments. I'd be mid-sentence—on a call, in a meeting, at dinner—and suddenly, for half a second, I'd see them.

The safe one. The bitter one. The one who stayed. The child who screamed in languages that didn't belong to him. They'd stand just behind my shoulder, not speaking. Just watching. A flicker, gone before anyone else could notice. But I noticed and I knew what it meant. They weren't dead. They were circling. And every time they came, they stayed a little longer. The more I tried to work, the more they pressed forward.

The characters I thought I had created weren't characters anymore. They were channels. They were old identities wearing new names, new costumes, trying to trick me into letting them live again.

They'd whisper in stolen voices:

"You didn't kill us. You only wrote around us." "We're still here."
"And you're still us."

The days got harder to track. Time became elastic—sometimes rushing, sometimes dragging, but always pulling me deeper into something I couldn't escape. I started reaching for anything that could slow the fall. Not escape. Not pleasure. Just… stabilisation.

Little rituals. Obsessive searches for information. Endless research spirals I couldn't quit. Every open tab, every book, every article felt like one more handhold to keep me from slipping fully into the void.

"If I can just learn more, understand more, find the missing piece, I'll be okay."

That's what obsession tells you. That's what addiction feels like when it's not chemical. You convince yourself you're still in control because your fuel is knowledge, not poison. But the effect is the same. The deeper I dug, the more fragmented I became.

Conversations grew shorter. Phone calls went unanswered. Texts sat unread. The people who loved me began to give up.

"You're disappearing," one friend finally said. "You're not the person I knew."

And they were right. The terrifying truth was I didn't miss who I was.

I didn't crave the old version of me anymore because some part of me was starting to believe that maybe this is what I had been evolving toward all along:

A pure machine of obsession.

The versions I thought I'd buried were no longer returning as whispers. They were inside me again; full-weight. Familiar voices with nowhere left to hide. At times, I would lose entire minutes—conversations I couldn't recall having.

Days blurred. Memories warped. There were moments where I'd hear myself speaking and not recognise the voice. Like watching a stranger use my face.

One night—and I can't say how long ago it was—I caught myself standing in the living room, lights off, staring at nothing. I wasn't thinking. I wasn't planning. I wasn't even afraid. I was simply absent. Not sleeping. Not awake. Just… paused.

Frozen inside a collapsing system that no longer knew which version of me was supposed to be driving. And for the first time, a new thought entered: "What if there's nothing left to fix?"

The final collapse didn't feel like breaking. It felt like vanishing. It wasn't an explosion. It wasn't even pain. It was absence.

The terrifying kind where you're fully awake, fully aware, and yet you feel yourself dissolving into something weightless. As if all the scaffolding you'd built to hold yourself up—the writing, the work, the rituals, the obsession simply gave out beneath you.

One moment I was standing. The next, I wasn't sure if I was even inside my body anymore. I don't remember how long it lasted. Hours? Minutes? Time becomes irrelevant when you're falling inward like that. There was no fear. No sadness. Just a sick, cold nothingness. A hollow state of being where even the versions inside me fell silent.

They weren't whispering anymore. They weren't pressing at the edges. They had already won. They were simply waiting because...what was left? Nothing. Not me. Not anyone. Just the vessel.

I heard my own voice—soft, detached, distant: "I don't know who I am anymore." And I meant it. It wasn't some dramatic crisis of identity. It was simple truth. I had outlived every version of myself. Killed them. Buried them. Obsessed over them. And now, standing alone in the ruins, I finally understood there was never supposed to be a final version.

The purge was never about survival. The obsession was never about truth. The work was never about art. It was always about erasure.

The reckoning wasn't coming. It had already happened. And I was still here. Somehow still writing, still bleeding, still pretending the aftermath was a process instead of a punishment. I didn't need saving. I needed permission to admit I'd already lost something I couldn't name. And maybe this page, this sentence, this breath, isn't a resurrection. It's just the echo of the man who stayed.

CHAPTER 6
THE SURVIVOR

"The versions I buried were never gone. They were only silent, waiting for me to have the courage to listen."

Hope is a dangerous thing
when you keep planting it in graves.
He did it anyway,
as if the dead might grow.

I was still here, though I couldn't quite explain why. There was no sense of victory in it. No clean redemption arc, no heroic climb out of the hole I'd dug. I hadn't fought my way back; I hadn't clawed my way through some dramatic final confrontation. What was left of me stood upright simply because there was no one else left to replace me.

The versions had gone quiet. The purge had done its work, at least for a time. The reckoning had stripped everything down to the most basic form of existence, and now I was left inhabiting a shell that vaguely resembled the man I used to be. I moved through familiar spaces—my home, the streets I knew, the routines I had built—but it all felt hollow, like walking through an abandoned house where the structure remained, but everything inside had been gutted by fire.

Mornings were the most jarring.

Each day blurred into the next. The world outside me carried on, indifferent to my hollowing. Emails still arrived. Phone calls were made. Colleagues continued their work. Friends, perhaps out of habit, still texted to check in. On the surface, everything looked intact. But I no longer felt inside of any of it. I answered when I had to, smiled when it was expected, spoke the appropriate words at the right times. And yet, as I did, I felt as though I was watching someone else wear my face and perform my life.

The writing had stopped. That was perhaps the most jarring shift of all. After years of being driven, possessed, and consumed by words, after years of being haunted by characters who demanded to be written into existence, there was now nothing. No voices. No scenes pressing forward. No scraps of dialogue rattling in my mind. The silence should have brought peace. But it didn't. It brought something far more unsettling and that was emptiness. Not even a grieving emptiness. Just absence. A dull hum beneath my skin, a low frequency I couldn't tune out. It wasn't painful. It wasn't loud. It simply was.

In that silence, a thought began to surface. One I had kept buried during all the years of noise. One I hadn't dared to fully acknowledge until now. It came gently, almost kindly, but carried with it the cold weight of something irreversible.

If I were still here, after everything I had destroyed, after every version of myself I had killed or left behind, then who exactly had survived?

There was a strange comfort in the hush, but it didn't last. As the days unfolded, something else began to emerge beneath the emptiness. It wasn't panic or the sharp, aggressive weight of collapse that had driven me before. This was slower, quieter. It came like a low fog curling in around my feet—guilt, creeping up from the places I had tried to seal off.

I began remembering them—not the characters, not the scripts or the storylines—but the versions. The ones I had killed off, rewritten, or abandoned along the way. Versions of myself I once wore like skin, some for years, some for moments. And though I had spent so much time convincing myself they had been necessary casualties in pursuit of the work, in this stillness, their absence no longer felt like progress. It felt like loss.

I found myself revisiting old journals, scraps of notebooks, files stored deep inside my hard drives. Notes I had written during the worst of it—small confessions I had long forgotten, fragments of thought scrawled late at night when I was still pretending to be in control. I read them now as if they belonged to someone else. Someone I barely recognised. Someone who had been trying to stay alive by any means necessary.

The guilt didn't scream. It whispered. It crept through the cracks I hadn't noticed until now. Not just guilt for what I had done to myself, but guilt for the people I had pushed away, the relationships I had drained, the conversations I never fully showed up for. They had been reaching for me all along, and I had been too deep inside my own collapse to reach back.

But the sharpest guilt of all wasn't for them. It was for the versions.

The dead versions of me.

I had killed them so ruthlessly believing it was necessary, believing it was survival. But now, standing here alone, I wasn't so sure. Each version I'd shed had carried pieces of me that felt painfully real—hopes, fears, regrets, small moments of clarity I could never reclaim. I had buried them with the belief that only one version could live. And yet here I was, wondering if I had been wrong all along.

A café receipt fluttered out—dated the week I quit baseball, margin-scribbled with a chapter title I never wrote. The guilt was tactile.

That was when I first felt the pull to write again. Not to create or to build a new story. But to speak, to confess everything I had committed. To them. Not the readers. Not the world. To the dead versions of myself who seemed impartial to wanting to be forgotten.

It began quietly, almost unconsciously. A blank page opened on my screen. My fingers hovered above the keys for a long time before I typed anything. And when I finally did, it came without hesitation, like opening a sealed wound.

"Dear version of me I couldn't save..."

The calm barely held. By afternoon the panic was back, a reminder that clarity is rented by the hour.

The words stared back at me from the screen, simple and honest in a way my writing hadn't been in years. There was no structure to this, no plan. I wasn't constructing narrative anymore. I was speaking directly into the graveyard I had built.

I sat there, breathing slowly, my fingers hesitant but steady. For the first time in a long time, I wasn't writing for anyone. Not for a reader. Not for the industry. Not even for the characters I had once given life to. This was for them—the pieces of me that never made it this far.

The next words came easier.

"I buried you when I thought you were weak. When I convinced myself, you were holding me back. I stood above your grave and told myself it was necessary. That only one of us could survive. And for a long time, I believed it."

I paused, my eyes scanning the page. It felt strange to see the confession there in black and white, as if admitting it finally gave form to something I had kept sealed for years.

"But I was wrong."

The sentence felt heavier than I expected. My chest tightened as I typed, like each word carried the weight of all the unspoken things I had refused to face. There was no one to edit this, no one to judge it. This wasn't for publication. This was something else. Something far more sacred.

"You weren't weak. You were unfinished. And I was too afraid to let you grow into who you might have become."

I could feel something shifting as I wrote—something loosening inside me, as if I was finally speaking to the ghosts properly for the first time. Not to silence them. Not to purge them. But to acknowledge their place in my survival.

"I didn't fail because you were too soft. I failed because I was too scared to carry you forward. I wore you like a costume, then stripped you off when I grew uncomfortable. But you were real. You were always real."

The words kept coming, steady, deliberate, as though they had been waiting years for me to finally give them breath. Each sentence felt like a funeral and a reconciliation all at once.

"I wonder sometimes what would have happened if I had let you stay. If I hadn't rushed to cut you loose. If I had allowed you to evolve instead of executing you the moment you made me uncomfortable."

The room around me was still. The only sound was the soft hum of the computer and the faint tapping of my keys as I kept writing. I hadn't intended to say this much. I hadn't even planned to write at all. But now that the words were coming, they refused to stop.

"I told myself you were dead weight. That you couldn't handle what was required. That I needed sharper edges, fewer feelings, fewer doubts. But you carried things I didn't want to face. You carried the parts of me that still believed in gentler things—hope, maybe. Vulnerability. The possibility that I didn't have to bleed to create."

I swallowed hard, my hands tightening briefly over the keyboard. There was an ache in my chest I hadn't felt in a long time—not panic, not fear. It was grief. Slow, steady, and overdue.

"I didn't bury you because you were useless. I buried you because you were too honest."

The words hit harder than I expected. I paused, staring at the screen, reading them repeatedly. There was something brutal about confronting my own cruelty—not toward others, but toward myself. The ruthlessness with which I had stripped away these versions in the name of discipline, of obsession, of control.

"You deserved more time. More space. A chance to exist fully, not as a stepping stone to something else. And now all I can offer you is this small apology, far too late."

I could feel the weight of it pressing into me, but instead of recoiling, I let it sit there. Let it settle. For once, I didn't try to solve it. I didn't reach for a narrative. I simply sat with the truth.

"You were part of me. And I'm sorry I made you believe you weren't enough."

The blinking cursor waited, patient and silent. The letter wasn't finished. There would be more. Many more. The graveyard was full of versions waiting for their turn. Waiting to be acknowledged. Waiting for me to finally stop killing them and start listening.

The next letter came the following night.

There was no ritual to it. No ceremony. The urge would arrive quietly, often late, often when the house was still and the world around me had surrendered to sleep. The emptiness I had once feared now became a strange kind of invitation—a space where I could finally sit with them, one by one.

I opened a new page.

"Dear version of me who pretended it didn't hurt..."

The words came quickly this time, as though he had been waiting closest to the door.

"You wore confidence like armour. You smiled in rooms where you didn't belong. You made jokes, changed the subject, and laughed loud enough to drown out the fact that you were breaking inside. You learned early that strength was performance. That no one would ask questions if you acted like you had the answers."

The words tasted bitter as I typed them. I remembered him so clearly—the version who could walk into any room, light it up, control the conversation, and make sure no one ever saw what was happening underneath.

"You kept everyone at a safe distance. You were charming. You were composed. You convinced even me that you were fine."

I paused, fingers hovering over the keys.

"And I let you carry that weight alone for far too long."

I felt my breath catch in my chest. This was different from the previous letter. This wasn't the version I had hated. This was one I had depended on—the one who kept me afloat while everything else inside me was falling apart.

"You weren't the lie. You were the shield. And I should have thanked you before I cut you loose."

I sat back, feeling the ache roll through my body again. This wasn't writing anymore. This was excavation. And there were many more layers to dig through.

Two nights later, another version appeared.

"Dear version of me who wanted to disappear..."

The words landed heavier.

"You were the one who thought silence would fix it. That if you stayed small enough, still enough, maybe the pain would pass by without seeing you. You mastered invisibility. You hid in plain sight. You stopped asking for help because you learned what it felt like when help never came."

I stared at the screen for a long time. This version was harder to face. He wasn't performative. He wasn't armoured. He was numb. Passive. The one who learned that surrender was safer than failure.

"You were tired long before I admitted it. And I hated you for that. I called you weak because I was terrified of how familiar your silence felt."

I exhaled slowly, my hand resting over my chest as if trying to quiet the rising heaviness there. These weren't characters. These weren't creative exercises. These were the ghosts I had carried through every stage of my obsession, and now they were finally being given a voice.

"I abandoned you because you reminded me how close I was to breaking."

The cursor blinked at me again. Always patient. Always waiting for me to find the courage to keep going. I closed the laptop that night knowing there would be more letters to write. The graveyard was deeper than I thought. But for the first time, I wasn't digging to kill anything. I was digging to bring them back—one version at a time. To give them space. To honour their existence. I wasn't sure yet what would happen when I reached the bottom. I only knew that I couldn't stop.

Not this time. The next letter arrived without warning. It was late. The house was silent again, as it always seemed to be now. I had started to crave these hours—not for peace, but for permission. The day belonged to performance, but the night belonged to truth. And I knew the next version had been waiting. I opened the document.

"Dear version of me who tried to fix everything..."

Even typing it felt exhausting.

"You were the one who couldn't sit still. Who believed that if you just worked harder, just learned more, just pushed a little further, maybe everything would finally stay in place.

You became an architect of control. Every schedule, every detail, every conversation carefully engineered to avoid chaos."

I paused, my jaw tightening as the words unfolded. This version had worked the hardest. He wasn't arrogant. He wasn't numb. He was desperate.

"You wore exhaustion like a badge of honour. People admired your discipline, your drive, your endless capacity to push through. And you clung to that praise like oxygen, because as long as you were producing, no one could see how close you were to falling apart."

My fingers hovered again. This one hurt more than the others.

"You thought control was safety. But all you were doing was delaying collapse. You were building a dam that was always going to break."

I let the sentence sit there. My chest tightened as I kept reading it back to myself. He wasn't wrong. He had done exactly what I asked him to do—he held it all together for as long as he could. Until I was ready to burn him, too.

"You were never weak. You were terrified. And I should have told you that was allowed."

For the first time in years, I felt the sting of tears in my eyes. Not the violent kind that ripped through you in grief or rage. But the quieter kind that simply arrive because you've finally stopped lying to yourself.

I leaned back in my chair, breathing slowly, letting the emotion settle. This was what survival actually looked like. Not the purge. Not the high. Not even the reckoning. It was this—sitting alone with my own ghosts, finally listening.

There were still more letters to write. And somewhere inside me, I understood:

This was always where the real work was waiting.

Another letter formed before I even opened the document. This one had been hovering closer than the others. I could feel him pacing for days, waiting for me to finally face him.

I began typing, slower this time.

"Dear version of me who needed to be important..."

The words tasted bitter before they even landed on the page.

"You were the one who believed that being loved wasn't enough. That you needed to be recognised. To be seen as special. To matter. And you chased that feeling into everything you touched—your work, your relationships, your ambition. The validation became its own kind of oxygen."

I felt my hands tightening on the keys. This was the version I least wanted to admit existed.

"You convinced yourself that your worth was tied to what you could produce. To how others saw you. To the weight of your ideas, your discipline, your sacrifices. The story was always bigger than the life behind it, and you clung to that illusion until you didn't know how to separate one from the other."

The shame arrived as I wrote. Slow at first, then thick and choking.

"You made art out of suffering, but what you really wanted was to be seen. To be told you mattered. And when the work wasn't enough, you blamed yourself for not bleeding more."

I stopped, swallowing hard. This version wasn't desperate. He was hungry. The kind of hunger that never lets you rest. The hunger that convinces you that no amount of success is ever truly enough.

"I fed you like a goddamn addict. And I called it passion."

The tears this time were sharper. Not grief. Not guilt. Just brutal honesty cutting clean lines through my chest.

"You weren't broken. You were trying to fill a hole that had no bottom. And I made you believe it was noble."

I leaned back again, eyes burning, chest hollow.

"I'm sorry. You deserved to be loved for who you were. Not for what you could build."

The words blurred on the screen as I sat there breathing. For years, I had been chasing something I couldn't name. And now, piece by piece, it was unfolding in front of me. This was never just about writing. This was never just about art. This was identity. Obsession. Compulsion. And now—finally—confrontation.

The next version didn't come quietly. He arrived like a weight dropping into my chest—a familiar heaviness I had carried in silence for far too long. I opened the page and sat for several minutes before typing.

"Dear version of me who almost didn't survive..."

The words came slower, like pulling heavy stones from deep water.

"You were the one who stopped pretending. The one who couldn't carry it anymore. When everyone else saw progress, you saw emptiness. When they called you strong, you felt hollow. You tried to hold it together for as long as you could, but the cracks were everywhere, and you were too tired to keep sealing them."

I paused, my breath shallow as the weight of the memory pressed against me.

"You weren't weak. You weren't broken. You were exhausted. You carried versions no one else ever saw, fought battles no one else ever understood. And when it became too much, you whispered to yourself what I never wanted to hear: 'I can't do this anymore.'"

The tears came fast now, sharp and clean. My fingers trembled as I kept typing.

"You were so close to disappearing. I remember the nights. The silence. The way the hours stretched into something bottomless. The way hope felt like fiction. And I remember how easy it would've been to let go. Just... let go."

The cursor blinked. My breath caught in my throat.

"But you didn't."

I closed my eyes as the truth landed hard.

"You stayed. Somehow, you stayed. Not because you believed things would get better, but because you didn't know what else to do. And I never thanked you for that. I never honoured you for the quiet fight you waged when no one was watching."

My chest heaved as I whispered the next words aloud, barely able to see the screen through the tears.

"You saved my life. And I buried you anyway."

I sat there, shaking, letting the letter sit open, unfinished.

There would be more. There was always more. But for now, this version had finally been heard.

For several days after finishing that last letter, I avoided opening the document again. Not because I believed the work was finished, but because I finally understood something I hadn't allowed myself to see before—this would never truly be finished. The graveyard of versions I carried inside me wasn't finite. It stretched far deeper than even I had been willing to admit. Each version was layered beneath the next, some louder, some long buried, but none of them entirely gone.

Yet something had shifted.

The act of writing no longer felt like an exorcism. I was no longer dragging these versions into the light to kill them again. The need to control, to purge, to cleanse myself with brutal precision had faded. What replaced it was something quieter, but far more unsettling. I was beginning to recognise that these versions, as fractured and painful as they were, had each carried something I once needed. They hadn't been obstacles; they had been companions. Necessary. Functional. Sometimes even protective.

I had spent years slicing pieces of myself away, believing it was the only way forward. Every purge felt like progress, every sacrifice justified. I believed that shedding the weaker versions was a form of evolution—that by killing off who I had been, I was clearing the path for who I was supposed to become. But now, staring at the stillness that followed, I couldn't deny the truth settling heavily into my chest.

This wasn't failure. It wasn't victory. It was simply growth. Ugly, uneven, unromantic growth. The kind no one applauds, because it happens quietly, in private, with no witnesses. The kind of growth that costs more than it gives, at least for a while.

And somewhere beneath all of it, beneath the exhaustion, beneath the grief, beneath the countless versions I had sentenced to silence, a strange sensation began to take root—one I hadn't felt in years.

Compassion.

Not for anyone else. For myself.

It arrived carefully, like a guest unsure whether it was welcome. It didn't bring comfort. It didn't promise healing. It simply stood there, patient, allowing me to feel what I had spent years avoiding: that I had done what I could, and that sometimes surviving is uglier than anyone wants to admit.

I sat there for a long time, not writing, not thinking, just breathing inside the quiet. And in that stillness, a thought surfaced—simple, but profound in its clarity.

I hadn't been writing to save myself. I hadn't even been writing to purge. I had been writing to witness. To witness every fractured version that carried me to this moment. To finally sit with them, not as failures, but as necessary parts of the story.

In the days that followed, I returned to the letters, but not with the same urgency. The fever was gone. The desperation to confront and destroy had faded into something quieter. I was no longer at war with these versions. I was learning to sit with them.

Sometimes I would read back through the pages I had written, revisiting the conversations I had denied myself for so long. I saw their faces differently now. Not as threats. Not as weaknesses to be eliminated. But as fragments of something whole—unfinished, yes, but never unworthy.

The shame was still there, but it had softened. It no longer arrived as sharp blades but as a dull, steady ache. An ache that said: You did what you thought you had to do. You survived the only way you knew how.

At night, I would find myself speaking to them silently. Not in dramatic confession, but in small acknowledgments.

You were trying. I see that now.

The house was still. The world around me remained unchanged. But inside, something subtle was taking shape. I was learning to carry the weight differently. Not lighter, necessarily, but with more honesty. Less denial.

I knew this wasn't the end of the work. There were more versions to face, more truths to unpack. But I no longer feared the process. The collapse had already taken what it could. What remained was not some purified version of me, but simply one that could finally stand still in the ruins without needing to justify its survival.

And for the first time in years, I closed my laptop without dread. Not because the work was finished—but because I had finally accepted that the work would always be part of me.

The purge was over. The reckoning had passed. And now, for the first time, there was space. Not emptiness. Space. Enough space to begin asking a different kind of question.

What comes after survival? After the illusion that balance is survival's reward?

CHAPTER 7
THE ILLUSION OF BALANCE

"I thought I was finally balanced. But I had only grown better at hiding the weight."

Some memories don't age.
They wait in corners like children,
asking if it's safe to come home yet.
He never answered.

For a while, things looked normal again. On the surface, at least.

I was sleeping a little more. Eating with some regularity. The bursts of obsessive writing had slowed to a more "manageable" rhythm. I told people I was doing better, and I meant it. Or at least I thought I did.

There were no more 3 a.m. spirals. No more letters written in blood-soaked memory. The ghosts had quieted, or so I believed. I wasn't haunted anymore. I was "centred." Focused. Still enough to function.

But underneath that stillness was something more dangerous than collapse. A lie I believed.

I convinced myself I had come through it all. That I had done the work. Survived the purge. Learned what I needed to learn. I started calling the chaos "the past," as if naming it that way meant it no longer had power.

I began rebuilding. Slowly, carefully. Reaching out to people I had pushed away. Finishing projects I'd left half-formed. Getting "back to life," as they say.

From the outside, I imagine I looked impressive. Grounded. Productive again. A man who had faced the abyss and made it out the other side.

But the truth? I had just gotten better at hiding the weight.

I was still carrying it. I had simply tucked it into places no one could see. I wore it in my smile. In my routines. In the way I said "I'm good" without blinking. The wound hadn't closed—it had just stopped bleeding in public.

Balance, I learned, is often just another word for silencing the collapse long enough to function.

There were days I didn't write at all. Not because I had nothing to say, but because I didn't want to risk breaking the spell. I was terrified that if I went back in, even for a second, everything I had glued together would fall apart again. I didn't trust myself yet. Not fully. I still feared what I might find if I cracked the lid open again.

I missed it. God, I did.

What I was living now felt... curated. Smoothed out. Polished enough to present, but hollow underneath.

There was one night I remember in particular—I was lying in bed, scrolling through an old draft of a script I had written during the height of the spiral. A scene between two characters I barely remembered inventing. The dialogue hit me like a freight train. It was raw. Unhinged. But alive. And I remember thinking:

"I don't even know who wrote this." That scared me more than anything.

Because I realised then—that version of me might be gone. The one who had been willing to bleed for it. The one who didn't care how it looked. The one who would risk losing his mind just to get the line right.

And for the first time, I wondered if this new version—this "balanced" self—had come at too high a cost. Maybe the ghosts weren't gone. Maybe they were just waiting.

Watching. Waiting for me to admit that this version was no more stable than the rest. Only quieter. I tried not to think in timelines anymore.

At some point, it stopped mattering whether the collapse had happened last month or five years ago. I didn't care what draft of which project I had been working on when things began to shift. That's the thing about writing the way I did—about living this way. Time stops being linear. The chapters don't unfold in sequence. They overlap. Loop. Fold into each other. One version of me writing, another dying, another waiting to be born.

It wasn't a biography I was writing. It was a dimensional record.

Every time I entered the world of story—particularly with Revelations—it was like stepping sideways into another life. Not metaphorically. Physically. My body would still be in the room, but my attention was somewhere else entirely. That realm, whatever you want to call it—the dimension of the story—became more real to me than the job I was doing to pay the bills. More vivid than my surroundings. More urgent than whatever life I was pretending to keep together.

I stopped measuring time by hours. I started measuring it by how deep I had gone.

People would ask how I was. I'd say I was "busy." That I was "getting through it." But the truth was, I was living two lives—and the one I kept disappearing into was the one that made the most sense. The only one that gave me a real sense of purpose.

That's what people didn't see. The toll wasn't just a lack of sleep or strained relationships—those were symptoms. The real toll was perspective. Everything outside the story lost weight. It didn't matter how well I performed in my job. It didn't matter if I got the part or booked the audition. It didn't even matter what was for dinner. I had crossed into a state of being where those things felt like someone else's obligations.

My purpose had rearranged itself.

I didn't want to be someone anymore. I wanted to write the truth—even if it meant obliterating the version of me that once needed validation from baseball, from acting, from external identity.

I began to feel like a detective. Not a literal one. A spiritual one. Chasing down the stories of the forgotten. The unspoken. The unnamed griefs inside people that no one had ever written for. It was as though I was tasked with finding out what happened to the missing parts of humanity—to the Jane and John Does that lived in memory and silence.

I couldn't just write casually anymore. I couldn't just "have an idea." I had to go under.

It took time—sometimes an hour, sometimes three—just to reach the place where my thoughts started talking to each other like they used to. I had to paddle out into it. Let the surface noise fade. Let the world recede. Only then did the writing come.

And when it came, it wasn't gentle. It took over the room. And then it got darker.

Because the stories I started writing didn't feel like inventions anymore. They felt... remembered.

Not from this life. Not consciously. But viscerally. Like the dreams you wake up from and can't shake for days, even though you don't know why. Like bruises you don't remember getting but still throb when you touch them.

I became obsessed with real victims. Real cases. The ones that didn't make the headlines. The missing. The discarded. The nameless girls in coroner's reports. The anonymous John Does on cold case forums. I read every detail I could find—not out of morbid curiosity, but out of some twisted sense of duty. I felt like I owed them something.

And slowly, they started to speak.

Not literally. But emotionally. Psychically. I'd be mid-sentence, writing a scene, and suddenly I'd feel an overwhelming urge—a grief, a panic, a memory that wasn't mine. A voice that didn't belong to any of my characters. It would hit me like static in the chest, like someone had just walked into the room with me and wanted to be heard. I began to think like a detective. But not a fictional one.

I wasn't solving stories anymore. I was living inside their timelines, trying to feel out what had happened. Sometimes I'd walk through a scene I was writing like I was conducting a crime scene reconstruction—imagining not what the character saw, but what she saw. The real girl. The lost one. The silenced one.

And when I say "real," I mean it. I felt her. Her pulse. Her terror. Her final thoughts. I would write it all down like a journal entry I had no right to remember. It was like I was becoming a ghostwriter for the dead and that did something to me I didn't expect. It made real life feel foreign.

There were moments I would be mid-conversation with someone—at work, or grabbing a coffee, or listening to a friend—and suddenly I'd feel myself drifting. Not out of boredom, but because a scene was building in my head. A scene I had to capture. I'd nod and smile and pretend I was still present, but in my mind, I was watching a woman run barefoot through industrial waste in the middle of the night. I could see the texture of the gravel slicing her feet. I could hear the way she gasped when the headlights found her.

The story was always louder than the room I was standing in. That made things hard to explain. How do you tell someone, "Sorry, I wasn't listening—a fictional murder victim was just whispering her final thoughts to me"? You don't. You smile. You pretend you're tired. You blame work. You say, "I've just got a lot on."

But then there were times when that silence cracked open in the real world—and someone stepped through it.

I remember one night, quite some time ago, after a speaking event to a group of creatives. A group of us were out having drinks, still riding the adrenaline of our night. It was light, casual. The kind of evening where you're expected to smile a lot and keep the conversation floating at surface level.

But then I found myself in a corner of the bar, speaking with a woman I'd never met before. She asked about my work. I hesitated at first—not everyone wants to hear about fictional dead girls and psychic collapses—but something told me to share it anyway. So, I did. I told her about the trilogy. About Revelations. About the way characters didn't just speak to me, they inhabited me. About the victims who kept showing up—not for plot, but for voice.

She went quiet.

And then, with this slight tremble in her voice, she told me she was the head of the state's Special Victims Unit—the real one. The one that deals with the worst cases. The stories no one wants to believe are true. She told me she couldn't believe we had just met, and that I had to finish this film. That it was needed. That it was echoing something she'd spent her whole career trying to bring into the light.

It shook me. And it wasn't the only time.

Around that same period, I found myself connecting with people in unexpected places—sometimes online, sometimes briefly in real life—and almost always, without me saying a word about my work, they'd open up. Women, strangers, confiding that they had lived through horrors they'd never told anyone. So many of them. One after the other. Different names, different cities, same story. Most of them still hadn't found a way to talk about it out loud. And yet they told me. As if, somehow, they knew I already understood.

And every time I shared what I was writing, what I was trying to build—it was the same reaction.

"You have to make this. You have to give this story a voice."

And in those moments, I didn't feel haunted anymore. I felt chosen. Like all the madness, all the breakdowns, all the characters I'd carried… it wasn't just for me. It was for them. For the ones who never got to whisper. For the ones still waiting to be heard.

But really, what you've got on is a full mental courtroom in session, a detective reconstructing the unspeakable, a family grieving in your head that doesn't even exist, and a killer whose voice you've almost perfected.

It's no wonder I stopped feeling real. It's no wonder I lost my place in the everyday. Because the truth was—I didn't want it anymore. I wanted the silence. The page. The whisper. The trace evidence of someone who never got justice. The chance to speak for them, even if no one was listening.

And that's when I knew…

This wasn't balance. This was immersion. And I was drowning with my eyes wide open. I didn't have a breakdown. I didn't disappear or collapse in the way people expect when they think of "losing yourself." I just got tired.

Tired of being a vessel for pain without ever asking why. Tired of chasing ghosts without knowing what they were trying to say. Tired of bleeding truth onto the page only to close the laptop and feel nothing but cold.

I didn't want to quit writing. I just didn't want to keep doing it like this.

There was one night—no different from the rest, really—where something shifted. I was reading over one of the old Dead Versions letters, one of the raw ones, the kind that sounded like a suicide note if you didn't understand what I was doing. It was written to the version of me that fell short. The one who almost made it but broke at the finish line. And as I read it, I remember whispering out loud:

"What was all this for?"

And not in anger. Not in despair. Just… genuine confusion. I had written hundreds of thousands of words. Created whole lives, buried entire versions of myself, lived in the skins of people who didn't exist—and I still didn't know what I was trying to prove.

I had spent so long trying to survive my own storytelling that I never stopped to ask if any of it mattered.

That's when it came—not an answer, but a pulse. A quiet certainty, like something leaning forward inside me for the first time.

"You have to make it matter now."

Not for a book deal. Not for followers. Not even for healing. But for the ones who never got to finish their story. The dead versions. The real ones. The imagined ones. The ones who were silenced in life or lost in fiction.

I didn't survive the spiral just to pretend it didn't happen. I survived to write about it with precision. To carve something clean out of something chaotic. To give a name to what so many others feel but can't articulate. To finally, finally begin turning all of it into something that served. Not just me. But anyone who ever felt like they were writing to outrun their own disappearance.

That's when the next phase began. The phase where I would stop purging the pain just to feel lighter…and start organising it into letters, into chapters, into a kind of personal mythology.

Not for closure. But for witness.

But the part that still unsettles me—the part I've only just begun to admit—is this:

What if some of those ghosts weren't mine?

What if, in the middle of all that creative possession, I became a vessel for other people's pain? What if, by listening too deeply, by opening too wide, I invited their dead versions in too?

It wasn't just that they told me their stories. It was the way they told them. The way they offloaded them. Sometimes with relief. Sometimes in tears. And then something shifted—in them, and in me. I watched them breathe differently. Smile. As if a weight had been passed along without either of us realizing it.

Maybe I became the place their ghosts could go.

Maybe they saw something in me—some hollow or fracture that looked like shelter—and they let their trauma move into me like squatters in a house under renovation. Not because they were careless. But because I let them. I opened the door. I always opened the door.

And if that's true...If even a handful of those stories latched onto my spine and stayed there, then maybe that's why I always felt so crowded in my own mind. Why the writing didn't just feel urgent, it felt congested. Why I kept breaking open even when I had nothing left to spill. Why I heard voices that didn't match my own pain but felt like mine anyway. Maybe some of the dead versions of me...weren't me at all.

And that's the danger no one warns you about: When you write from the wound, when you live in the fracture, you don't just lose yourself. You become a receptacle for the ghosts no one else had space to carry.

I didn't climb out. I didn't heal. I just started arranging the ruins into something that looked like a foundation. I stopped asking when it would end and started asking what it wanted from me. And for the first time in a long time, I wasn't writing to escape. I was writing to remember—who I had been, what I had lost, and who I might still have a chance to become… if I stayed with it long enough to listen.

CHAPTER 8
THE BECOMING

"Survival isn't the end of the story. It's the beginning of authorship. The ghosts didn't leave — they just stopped screaming when I started writing them down."

He was never chasing freedom.
He was just trying to find a version of himself
that could sit in silence
without shattering.

I didn't wake up one day and decide to rebuild. There was no sunrise epiphany. No neatly timed turning point. Just an exhausted kind of clarity, the kind that shows up when you're too tired to keep performing collapse. At some point, the screaming inside my head became background noise. At some point, the dead versions stopped asking to be saved. They started asking to be written. That's when I realised something had shifted.

I wasn't trying to escape anymore. I was trying to make sense. I wasn't trying to outrun the madness. I was trying to organise it. Name it. Shape it. Turn it into something that could survive me.

Because that's the thing no one tells you about becoming the vessel: once you've carried that much darkness, that much noise, you can't just go back to small talk and goal setting. You either keep carrying it... or you start pouring it into something that might mean something to someone else.

I didn't know what healing looked like. But I knew what listening looked like now. And so I started listening more carefully. To pauses and patterns and to the shape of my own silence. Because buried beneath all the chaos wasn't just trauma—there was intention and structure. There was something forming. And maybe... just maybe... if I stayed inside it long enough without breaking again, I could finally become more than a collection of ghosts.

There was a strange calm that followed once I stopped trying to fix everything. Not peace exactly, but a kind of resignation with purpose. I stopped needing every moment to be a revelation. I stopped needing to be "better." What I needed now was to understand—and understanding doesn't always come with light. Sometimes, it only arrives in shadow. So, I started mapping the wreckage.

Not to clean it up. But to know it better. To see which parts of me had been casualties, and which were still breathing. I would open old drafts, reread letters I'd written in the dark, so to speak. Pieces I'd almost deleted. Voice notes I'd recorded while driving at night, half-possessed by some character trying to get one last word in. It was like for the first time; I was meeting my own mind without trying to edit it.

And what I found surprised me. There were patterns. Repetition. Structure. Themes that echoed across different projects without me realising. The same wounds dressed up in different clothes. The same version of me dying again and again under a hundred different names. I had been writing the same story for years. Not because I lacked imagination—but because I hadn't finished living it.

That's what broke me open all over again. Not the trauma or the madness. It was the realisation that the work wasn't leading me to freedom. It was leading me to recognition. These weren't separate breakdowns. They were chapters. And I was finally starting to read them in order. That's when the letters changed.

They had always been instinctive. Hasty lines in notebooks, fragments of confession written in moments when I couldn't face a mirror. But now they became structured. Focused. Still raw, yes, but no longer chaotic. These weren't breakdowns anymore. They were eulogies. Blueprints. Warnings. Dead Versions of Me wasn't just a phrase anymore. It was a process.

Every letter became a form of emotional recordkeeping. A way to honour the versions of me that hadn't made it, and to name the ones I could feel slipping through my fingers. Some entries came calmly, like closing a chapter. Others came like self-exorcisms—blistering, unrelenting, violent in how much they wanted to be released.

I wrote to the boy who still thought success would fix him. To the man who sacrificed his needs just to feel needed. To the version of me that mistook survival for strength. To the one who held the pen so tight he forgot it could be a weapon or a wound. Each one had something to say.

Some forgave me. Some blamed me. Some just asked me to remember them before I buried them again. And I listened. Not to glorify the past. Not to swim in suffering. But to understand what had brought me here to this strange in-between place where I was no longer just breaking… I was becoming.

Becoming someone who could hold all of them without needing to dissolve. Someone who could look at the ghosts and say: You lived. You shaped me. But you're not the author anymore.

I thought that was it. That I had done enough. That the writing, the remembering, would be the cure. But ghosts don't care about closure. They care about witnesses. And as soon as I stopped burying them, they started standing up. I wasn't just writing the story anymore. I was being written into it. I thought I could handle it. All of it, inside my head.

Some people make vision boards. Others spill their chaos onto walls and whiteboards or line their living room floors with scribbled index cards. But not me. I kept everything internal. A collapsing library of timelines, names, letters, themes, echoes, deaths, rebirths—all stacked precariously in the corners of my mind like unstable furniture.

And I kept trying to make sense of it all.

Every night became a kind of internal autopsy. I'd lie in bed and mentally thumb through a hundred different characters, dozens of old files, forgotten voice memos. I'd cross-reference emotional arcs in my sleep. Wake up trying to remember what version of me had written which scene. I'd obsess over whether this line belonged to the man I had become, or the boy who never made it.

I told myself this was productive. That it was just my process. But it wasn't. It was a silent implosion.

The thoughts weren't neatly filed—they were stacking. Multiplying. Crushing the quieter parts of me. I'd try to trace a single character's origin and end up re-living entire relationships, dreams, versions of my past I had no business revisiting without armour. And each time I lost the thread, I blamed myself. For forgetting. For not being stronger. For not finishing the map I thought I was building.

The truth was: I wasn't mapping anything. I was drowning in every unfinished version of me I had tried to catalogue.

And worse—I started to feel like I was betraying them all. Like their voices were fading because I wasn't listening properly anymore. Because I wasn't doing them justice. Because I thought organising them would save me.

But ghosts don't want to be archived. They want to be acknowledged. And in that failure, in that collapse of my mental filing system, something cracked open. The letters weren't finished. The hauntings weren't over. And the past wasn't done with me yet.

CHAPTER 9
THE ALLUSION LETTERS

"I left behind versions of myself so convincing, I started believing them too."

PART I
THE KINDNESS OF MISUNDERSTANDING

DVOM

He stopped writing for the world.
Started whispering just to himself.
The silence didn't answer back,
but it listened.

There are things I wanted to say. Things I rehearsed a thousand times in the dark, letting the words build pressure behind my teeth like steam in a closed room. But they never made it out. Not because I was afraid, but because I already knew — you wouldn't have heard me anyway.

You think you listen, but you only ever hear what makes sense to you. I don't blame you. Most people are just trying to keep up with the noise of their own lives. But still, it leaves people like me speaking a language no one recognizes. Not because it's complex, but because it's quiet. Too quiet for someone waiting for thunder.

You wanted declarations. You wanted clarity, drama, something digestible. But I've never lived in the clean lines of an argument or a perfectly timed response. I live in the hesitation before someone answers. I live in the breath someone takes when they're about to say something real, but swallow it instead. That's where I exist — in the emotional pauses no one notices.

I used to think being understood meant being loved. That if someone could map the geography of my pain, they'd finally know how to hold me. But somewhere along the way, I realised you weren't trying to see me. You were trying to solve me. And there's a difference.

You asked questions like a detective, not a friend. You dissected my sentences, looked for themes, waited for contradictions. You watched me like I was a story you hadn't finished reading yet — as if some final twist would explain why I am the way I am.

You thought I was mysterious. That was flattering for a while but mystery is only romantic until you realise it means people are only paying attention when you confuse them. Not when you're being soft. Not when you're being real.

You didn't want the truth. You wanted the puzzle. You wanted the sad boy narrative, the stormy eyes, the half-truths, the cigarette-smoking silhouette version of me you could tell your friends about. You didn't want the version who couldn't sleep for nights on end. Who shut down at dinner. Who cried in the car for reasons even he didn't understand.

You loved the metaphor of me. But you couldn't handle the man.

And in hindsight, maybe I let you get away with that. Maybe I only ever gave you the poetic parts. Maybe I was scared that the truth — the boring, bruised, stammering truth — wouldn't be enough. Or worse, that it would drive you away faster than the mystery ever could.

And so I became a riddle. Not a person. Just an allusion to one.

I tried to explain. I really did. But everything I wanted to say came out sounding like a metaphor. Like a riddle. And maybe that's because I never learned how to speak in facts. Only in feeling. And the moment I realised you were more interested in solving me than seeing me, I shut down.

You said I was distant. You said I was hard to read. But what you never saw was how loud it was inside me. You never noticed how much I had to mute just to show up in a way that didn't scare you off. That's the thing — people want vulnerability until it becomes inconvenient. Until it challenges them. Until it sounds like grief and not a poetic caption.

So I kept it all buried. Spoke in code. Nodded at the right times. And when you finally walked away, I didn't stop you. You thought I didn't care. But the truth is, I was just tired. Tired of asking to be understood by people who only ever wanted the version of me that made sense to them.

And now, here I am, writing this, not for you, but for the version of me that kept waiting for someone to read between the lines. He's gone now. Or maybe he's just quiet like he always was. Either way, you wouldn't recognize him. But I would.

And that's enough.

PART II
ECHOES WITHOUT EARS

DVOM

*There were still pieces of him scattered,
in places he didn't remember leaving them.
Some days, grief wore his name.
He wore it anyway.*

There was a time when I truly believed that the more I suffered, the more valuable I became. That pain gave me depth. That loneliness made me noble. That being fucked up was a sign of being chosen — like the universe handed me a more complex, tragic script than everyone else, and I was meant to carry it like some poetic martyr.

And people believed it, too. They'd say things like, "You've been through so much," with that look. You know the one. That mix of awe and sadness and quiet relief that they're not the one holding the grief. I started to wear my pain like a badge — subtle, of course. We can't look too self-important about it. But still. It made me feel like I mattered.

Because at least when I was suffering, I wasn't invisible. No one claps for contentment. No one marvels at your healing. No one stops scrolling for a man who's okay. But suffering? That has gravity. That gets attention. That gives you something to lean on when the rest of you has fallen apart. It lets you say things like, "They'll regret how they treated me when they realise what I've been through." And you start believing that everyone else's joy is ignorance, while your sadness is enlightenment. It becomes addictive.

Being misunderstood starts to feel like proof that you're deeper than everyone else. That they just can't handle your depth. That your pain is too nuanced, too intellectual, too earned. And that's the lie. That's the trap. Because eventually, you start guarding your suffering like treasure. You don't want to get better. You want to win.

You want your pain to mean something. You want it to make you someone. Because if it doesn't, then what the hell was it all for? The years of breaking down? The nights of disappearing into the ceiling? The way you drifted away from everyone who tried to reach you? If your suffering doesn't make you special... then maybe you were just hurting. Like everybody else.

And that's a brutal thought. Because it strips you of the narrative. The crown. The subtle ego trip that says, "No one's been through what I have." But they have. Maybe not in the same costume. But the story? The ache? The hollowing out of who you were supposed to be? Yeah. Others have lived that too.

And here's the truth that nearly undid me: Your pain doesn't make you more important. It just makes you real. I didn't want to be real. I wanted to be the broken hero. The sad poet. The man whose agony made him magnetic. I wanted applause for the ache. I wanted forgiveness without the work. I wanted to be understood without having to explain myself — because shouldn't my suffering be obvious by now? Turns out, it wasn't.

Turns out, no one's pain is that loud to anyone but themselves. So here I am, finally sitting in the middle of my story, knowing I'm not the main character of everyone else's. Knowing my suffering is not some holy currency. It doesn't entitle me to closeness. It doesn't make me wise. It just was. And maybe the sharpest blade isn't the pain itself. Maybe it's the way I used it to cut others away. To say, "You'll never understand me," instead of asking, "Would you try?"

Maybe I've been insensitive. Not because I couldn't feel. But because I wouldn't let anyone else feel with me. That's changing now. Slowly. Maybe.

PART III
THE CONFRONTATION

The ghosts didn't leave.
They just sat beside him quietly.
He learned to make room for them,
instead of digging more graves.

Let them think I'm cold. Let them think I shut down. Detached. Unreachable. Unbothered. It's easier that way. Because if you think I'm cold, you won't ask why I went quiet. You won't press your hand to the places I've numbed just to keep going. You'll just shake your head and walk away. And I won't have to explain that I didn't shut down because I didn't care. I shut down because I couldn't keep bleeding in front of people who only noticed the mess — never the wound.

I've learned that silence looks like arrogance when someone doesn't understand pain. I've learned that self-preservation can come off like cruelty if you've never had to hide how much something was killing you.

But here's the part no one sees; I used to try. I used to explain. I used to spell it out, syllable by syllable, hoping someone would meet me halfway. I used to open the door and let people in, thinking that vulnerability was the key to closeness. But then I learned what happens when you hand someone your truth and they look at it like it's an inconvenience. Like it's a burden. Like they've got somewhere else to be.

You learn to close the door. And then you learn to build a wall. And after a while, the wall isn't something you put up. It's just… where you live. I don't want to be cold. But when people expect you to be warm while they ignore the weather you're standing in, you stop offering comfort. You stop offering anything.

And they call you distant. They call you hard. They call you dramatic, or too much, or worse — nothing at all. Let them. Let them reduce what they never stayed long enough to understand. Let them turn your emotional surgery into a personality flaw. Because what they call "cold" was actually me, frozen in a moment I never got to finish.

A moment where I was cornered — by my own exhaustion. By the endless rerun of conversations where I asked to be seen and left with silence. No, I didn't disappear. I just got tired of watching people applaud my survival while ignoring the war it took to keep breathing. So I made it simple. I stopped needing to be known.

If I became the villain in their story, fine. If I became the "emotionally unavailable one," so be it. Because behind the walls, behind the chill, behind the carefully timed silences, is a version of me that doesn't need to be decoded. He just needs to be left the fuck alone long enough to remember who he was before they convinced him he was too much and not enough at the exact same time.

Let them think I'm cold. That's easier than telling them I used to be warm until warmth stopped being safe.

PART IV
THE MIRROR ISN'T FOR YOU
(GRIEF IS A MIRROR, NOT A MEGAPHONE)

For the first time,
he didn't apologize for the fire.
He let it burn,
not to destroy, but to begin.

I've stopped announcing my grief. Not because it left, but because it found a quieter place to live inside me. It's no longer a loud visitor banging at the front door — it's become part of the architecture now. A hidden room at the back of the house no one visits. I don't show it to guests. I don't keep it locked. But I do tend to it. I dust it off when it settles too deep. I pass through it when the air shifts. And sometimes, I sit there alone, with no words, letting it be what it is — unpretty, unfiltered, unanswered.

Grief, I've come to realise, doesn't always wear tears on its face. Sometimes, it disguises itself as everyday forgetfulness — like losing your keys, then sitting on the floor for twenty minutes, not because you're confused, but because you're too tired to keep looking. Sometimes, it echoes in laughter that doesn't sound quite right. Sometimes, it's that half-second pause before answering a simple question like, "How've you been?" The delay where your soul scans for the version of you that still knows how to answer honestly.

I used to believe grief had to be loud to be real. That it needed ceremony. Rituals. That it came with final letters and brave last words. That it showed up dressed in black, commanding silence and sympathy. But the most honest kind of grief I've known is the kind no one sees but me. The kind that doesn't beg for witness. The kind that waits until your guard is down. When you're rinsing a plate, folding laundry, then taps you gently on the shoulder, like a child wanting to be held.

It doesn't need applause. It doesn't crave attention. It doesn't even want to explain itself. It just wants a seat at the table. Even if it never speaks.

People say, "You have to let go," as if grief is a balloon. As if release is the holy act. As if the hands that still hold something must be weak or unwilling. But I don't always believe in that kind of letting go. Sometimes, I think holding on is the braver thing. Not to the pain itself — not to the ache or the story of the loss — but to what the pain stood for. The connection. The piece of you that only existed when that person, that hope, that dream, was still breathing.

Letting go might bring peace. But holding on quietly, without spectacle might be love.

And still, we live in a world that confuses performance with processing. If you don't talk about it, post about it, package it with a caption, it's like it didn't happen at all. As if silence is denial. As if healing only counts when it's witnessed.

But what about the ones who grieve without a stage? The ones who break in silence. Heal in pieces. The ones who carry their memories like pocketed glass — never displayed, but always near?

That's the grief I know. The grief that doesn't need to prove itself. The kind that doesn't need a funeral song or a eulogy. The grief that stays, quietly, even when no one's watching.

And when I look in the mirror, it's still there. Not drowning me. Not dragging me under. Just sitting beside me. Like an old friend who doesn't need to talk. Like a truth that no longer needs permission to stay. Not a megaphone, but a reflection. Proof that something mattered. Proof that something was real. Even if no one else saw it but me.

PART V
THE EMPATHY OLYMPICS

He stopped chasing endings.
Started tracing the thread between versions,
Realising none of them were wasted;
Only waiting.

Welcome to the arena.

This is where suffering gets scored. Where pain is no longer a private experience, but a performance art. And in this game, everyone's trauma is valid — but if we're honest, mine is just a little more poetic, a little more deserving, a little more branded for the algorithm.

Points are awarded for childhood wounds, especially the kind you've turned into captions. For toxic relationships — extra if you kept the screenshots and even more if you posted them with vague, lyric-heavy quotes. You'll gain traction for taking a "mental health day," but only if you style it properly: soft colours, a flat lay of self-care items, maybe a close-up of a hand loosely holding tea.

We celebrate crying in cars now — as long as there's a vintage overlay and the lighting hits just right. Diagnoses? You don't need to understand them. Just pick one that matches your aesthetic this month. Something raw, mysterious, tragic-but-beautiful.

And yes, there are bonus points. Cry on camera without ruining your eyeliner — and you're a champion. Speak about your healing journey without ever naming what actually broke you? That's double points.

But be warned. The line is fine. Say too much, and you're desperate. Say too little, and you're cold. Sound confident? You're self-absorbed. Seem unsure? You're unstable. Too healed? You're faking it. Too broken? You're a burden.

The trick is to stay just broken enough not to be damaged, but digestible. Vulnerable, but still photogenic. Wounded, but in a way that won't make anyone look away. Because none of this is really about getting better, is it? It's about being seen *trying* just enough to stay relevant. Just enough to be relatable. Just enough to be admired and pitied at the same time, but never enough to make people uncomfortable. God forbid you make someone uncomfortable with your realness.

And I'll be honest with you, I've played this game too. I've curated my pain. I've sanded down the messy edges and given it a filter. I've used it to justify my distance, to make myself seem complicated and mysterious — when really, I was just hurt. I was tired. And I was quietly hoping someone would ask how I actually felt... without me needing to post about it.

Because real empathy, the kind that sits beside you and doesn't flinch, the kind that doesn't try to fix you or repurpose your grief into something marketable, that's rare now.

What we have instead? It's emotional currency. And everyone's trading it like stock.

"Look how deep I am."
"Look how raw I can be."
"Look at my growth."
"Look how beautifully I fall apart under soft lighting."

But this isn't connection. It's theatre. It's not healing. It's branding. We've taken grief and turned it into content. We've built entire identities out of suffering and made pain a fucking aesthetic. And here's the part no one wants to admit: some people don't actually *want* to get better. Because healing means losing the thing that made them interesting. It means becoming whole and maybe boring. And boring doesn't get shared. Boring doesn't go viral.

But you want to know what's worse than all that? I used to envy them. I used to look at the ones who were comforted, the ones whose sadness pulled people closer instead of driving them away and I thought they were the lucky ones. The chosen. The ones whose ache made them worthy of love.

Their pain became a passport. A reason for people to stay. A character trait. And I wanted that. But I see it now. I see what it really is. It's hollow.

All of it.

Because real healing is not cinematic. It's not framed in good light or timed with music. It's boring. It's quiet. It's repetitive. It's waking up every day and showing up for yourself when no one notices. It's crying in a room no one sees and still finding the strength to keep going. Not for attention. Not for clout. Not for applause.

Just because you finally believe you're worth it. It's not a post. It's not a reel. It's not a badge. It's not a caption that wraps it all up neatly. It's not winning anything.

And I'm done.

I've disqualified myself. I've stepped out of the arena. Let someone else win the gold medal in performative pain. I'm finished pretending that trauma makes me more important. Finished pretending that staying broken earns me belonging. I'd rather be boring and real than brilliant and broken for show.

PART VI – A
WHEN THE PAST BECOMES POSSESSIVE

He wrote without bleeding.
Spoke without shaking.
For once, the mirror didn't flinch.
And neither did he.

I stopped visiting the past the moment it started answering back.

And not in a nostalgic way—not the kind that welcomes you in with old laughter and warmth or shows you how far you've come. No, this was different. It began speaking like an old friend with a grudge, one that remembered every detail you didn't want to carry anymore. And the more I listened, the more I realised this wasn't guidance—it was manipulation dressed in memory.

Have you ever felt that strange sensation, like you're being misled by your own former self? As if there's a version of you from the past—seemingly well-meaning, maybe even wise—trying to lead you forward, only to quietly steer you back into the same small circles you fought so hard to escape? That version doesn't scream. It just speaks louder in quiet moments, persistent and persuasive, offering you the safe bet every time. Stay still. Play it small. Don't risk it. Remember what happened last time?

The line I wrote at the start—*"I stopped visiting the past the moment it started answering back"*—that wasn't just a quote to fill a caption. That was the moment the story broke. The narrative snapped in half. That was the fracture point. The rebellion. When I realised that not all memories are sacred, and not every version of myself deserves to live on.

There's a difference between honouring who you were and being haunted by him. Some versions don't want healing. They want control. They don't care if you evolve, or grow, or love again. They just want you stuck. Apologising for what you've already survived. Living inside a loop of old shame and expectations.

It's a strange thing to witness in others, too. You see it in their eyes. In their habits. In the way they fight battles that no longer exist—ghosts with outdated weapons. It's almost a bizarre sight, watching someone argue with the dreams of yesterday. Watching them gather rusted memories and broken identities like ammunition, hoping they can still defend themselves in a world that's long since changed shape.

But you can't win a war with old machinery.

And yet... there's a sadness that creeps in alongside this clarity. Because the past doesn't go quietly. It doesn't just surrender and slip away with grace. Sometimes, it begs. Sometimes, it becomes bitter. There's an emotional violence in realising that the former you—the one who tried, who held on, who believed—isn't needed anymore. That version doesn't die a noble death. He's retired. Silenced. Replaced.

And that hurts more than I expected.

It reminds me of something deeper, something even more human: the way a parent must feel when their child no longer needs them. Not for food. Not for advice. Not for safety. Just... not at all. When the child walks out into the world and the parent is left behind, watching, waiting, trying not to ask the question that's forming anyway: *Am I still useful?*

That's how the old versions of ourselves die—not in ceremony, but in absence. Not because they did something wrong, but because time moved on. It's not rejection, exactly. It's obsolescence. And it is, in many ways, a soul-destroying kind of grief.

Still, we have to ask: why do we shed them at all?

Why must we kill off yesterday's self in order to step into tomorrows? Why can't we just… carry them with us?

The truth is—we can. We do. In ways we don't always recognise. We relive them when we smell something familiar or hear a song we didn't know we'd forgotten. We revisit those moments through the way we raise our children, through the rituals we inherit, through the questions we still ask late at night when no one's around to answer.

I look at my son—he's almost fifteen now—and I still see every version of him stacked inside the boy he is today. I can hear the baby he once was in his laughter, see the toddler in the way he stumbles through new experiences, still hungry for truth. Those memories don't fade. They fortify. They matter. They *are* me.

So no—I'm not here to erase the past. I'm not here to turn the old versions into villains. I'm just done letting them speak over my future.

They can sit beside me, sure. They can remind me. Warn me. Even weep a little if they need to. But they don't get the wheel. Not anymore.

I'll carry them with me. But I'm the one who decides where we go from here.

PART VI – B
WHEN THE PAST STARTS ANSWERING BACK

He wrote without bleeding.
Spoke without shaking.
For once, the mirror didn't flinch.
And neither did he.

For the longest time, I believed the past was supposed to be quiet. I pictured it like an old, closed room in a house I no longer lived in—dust settling where no breath remained, memories folded into corners where the light no longer reached. I thought time would seal it off, gently and respectfully, as though healing was nothing more than a process of outliving the ache. But lately, I've come to understand that some rooms don't stay silent. Some doors swing open long after you've locked them, and sometimes, the past finds a voice.

It started subtly—like a forgotten tune threading itself back into my head while washing dishes, or the sudden sense that someone was standing behind me in an empty room. A flicker in the mirror. A familiar phrase echoing from someone else's mouth. At first, I brushed it off. The brain plays tricks, I told myself. This is just old wiring misfiring. But it didn't stop there. It grew bolder. Less suggestion, more statement. Less memory, more confrontation. The voice of my past—my own voice, really, warped and worn—began speaking in ways I couldn't dismiss.

It questioned the very foundation I was building. It told me the suffering I remembered might not have been as deep as I claimed. That perhaps I had framed myself as the wounded one to escape the guilt of what I didn't do—what I failed to say, who I failed to protect. It whispered that I had rewritten my own history not out of growth, but out of convenience. And the most disarming part of it all was that the voice didn't sound like an enemy. It sounded like someone who used to love me. Someone who still might, under different rules.

I had spent years writing about the past as if I were its master, as if I'd sorted it, named it, archived it with clinical precision. I made art out of it. I painted over the blood and called it metaphor. But now, I wonder if I ever laid anything to rest at all. Maybe I didn't bury the versions of me I claimed to. Maybe I just left them behind in locked rooms, and now they've grown restless with the silence. Maybe they're not ghosts. Maybe they're survivors too—ignored, bitter, and finally ready to speak.

And so they do.

Sometimes I hear them in mirrors, not in words but in weight—in the heaviness behind my own eyes, in the way my mouth tightens when I try to smile too early in the morning. Sometimes they follow me into conversations and twist my sentences before I speak to them. "You don't really mean that," they say. "You're just performing who you've become." Other times, they lay accusations in my lap so casually it takes me days to recognize the wound. You were never that strong. You didn't really heal. You're still that scared, soft-hearted kid—just better dressed now.

And I'll be honest: part of me listens. Not because I want to believe it, but because I know how much truth can hide beneath the sentences, we resist the most. These voices remember the parts of me I've avoided. They know every corner I cut. Every apology I never made. Every moment I chose silence over truth because it felt safer to seem okay than to actually face what wasn't.

For a long time, I told myself I had changed. But change, I've come to realise, is not the same as evolution. You can rebrand your identity without ever actually touching the rot underneath. You can clean the surface so well that even you forget what's festering beneath it. The difference between healing and hiding is not always visible from the outside. But the past sees it. The past always sees it.

There is a kind of grief that comes with realizing you might still be editing your life for the comfort of others. Not living it. Not owning it. Just trimming the mess for readability. I've written chapters that were never true, but they sounded good. And in that way, I suppose I betrayed the version of me who once cried out just to be heard—not understood, not forgiven, just witnessed.

But I hear him now. I hear all of them.

And no, I'm not here to give them back control. I'm not collapsing under their weight. I'm not burning the progress I've made just to validate their return. But I'm also not pretending they aren't real. These old versions—they built this house. Some with bare hands, some with blood. They deserve a eulogy. Not a prison.

So let them answer back.

Let them tell their side. Let them scream in the dark corners if they must. Let them call me out on the ways I tried to move on without looking back. I will not run from them this time. I will not dress them up as metaphors or ghosts or poetic warnings. I will face them plainly, directly, without defence.

Because I don't need to be innocent to be whole. I don't need to erase my past to author my future. I just need to stop pretending that silence was ever the same thing as peace.

PART VII
THE PERFORMANCE OF HEALING

He didn't need to be believed anymore.
He only needed to believe himself.
That was louder than applause,
and softer than permission.

There's a kind of tired you don't get to talk about.

Not in rooms with good lighting. Not when people are rooting for you. It's not fatigue exactly. It's the cost of performing wellness, of staging the recovery before the wound has even scabbed. They call it strength, but some days it feels more like fraud. And you play along because you're afraid of what people might do if they saw the raw version, not the one who survived, but the one who's *still* bleeding under clean clothes.

You learn early how to wear a version of yourself that earns comfort from others. It doesn't take much. A few smiles. A joke that says, *"See? I'm okay."* And they nod. And you stay on stage. Because applause, even when undeserved, is easier than silence. I can't pinpoint the first time I got praised for hiding it. But I remember the *feeling*. The relief of being accepted, the subtle high of being seen as resilient. Like pain could be power if you just spoke it in past tense.

But here's the thing no one tells you: healing has a performance clause. It asks you to dress the part. It wants you articulate, composed, functional. It wants to see your pain filtered, formatted, processed. Not because it cares, but because *they* do. And they need your survival story to fit inside their attention span.

So, you clean it up. You make it palatable. You cry quietly, edit your honesty, and package your inner war as "growth." And slowly, almost invisibly, the distance between who you are and who you're pretending to be becomes unbearable.

There was a night, no loud collapse, no cinematic breakdown, just me sitting on the edge of the bed in a dark room where the air felt heavier than usual. The TV was still playing. Some rerun I wasn't watching. One sock on, one off. Hands locked together like they were trying to hold in something I didn't have the language for. I wasn't sad. I wasn't angry. I was just... *done performing.*

And I remember thinking: *If I break now, will anyone even notice? Or worse... will they cheer?*

It wasn't a cry for help. It was the whisper of someone who's been "strong" for too long asking permission to stop.

I've had moments behind doors no one will ever open, where I let the whole mask drop. No audience. No control. Just me, the ghosts, and whatever version of God hadn't walked out yet. I wasn't mourning an event. I was mourning the weight of always needing to be someone *after* the hurt. The pressure to be a writer of pain, not a human inside of it. And in that moment, I wasn't broken. I wasn't brave. I was just *honest.* And it felt like betrayal.

Because when you've built a version of yourself on being "the one who got through it," who do you become when you haven't?

There's a quiet rage in that. Not at people, not always. But at the expectation. At the way the world demands a blueprint of your healing so they can feel better about their own broken things. They want you to be the lighthouse, even when your own hands are still shaking from the shipwreck.

I catch myself now, mid-sentence, pausing to ask: *Is this real or rehearsed?* Sometimes I don't know anymore. The performance has become muscle memory. Smile. Respond. Be grateful. Move on.

But my son sees through that. He's fifteen now — old enough to mirror back what I haven't said. And sometimes, in his silence, I see the same performance beginning in him. A soft retreat. A knowing smile that hides too much. And I wonder, *did he learn that from me?*

Then a harder thought:

Who did I learn it from?

Because if I'm honest — I think I watched men before me do the same thing. My father. His father. A long line of locked jaws and tightened fists and "I'm fine" said with shoulders that were clearly not. And I wonder if all of us were just trying to die quietly enough that it wouldn't burden anyone.

Maybe that's the worst part of it.
Not the pain — but the inheritance of silence.

Because real healing — the kind that doesn't fit in a caption or a highlight reel — is *messy*. It's inconvenient. It doesn't care about timelines or redemption arcs. It shows up on days you need to be functional. It ruins your creative flow. It interrupts your dinner plans. It doesn't give a shit about your brand.

But it's real. And I'd rather be honest than impressive.

So, if you see me distant, or quiet, or a little harder to reach these days — don't assume it's regression. Maybe I'm just tired of being the exhibit. Maybe I've finally started giving myself permission to fall apart without documenting it.

Or maybe, I'm healing in the most powerful way of all: Without needing you to see it. There's a kind of tired that finally lets go of being tired. And maybe... that's the real healing after all.

PART VIII
THE ILLUSION OF CLOSURE

The story wasn't over.
It was just quieter than usual.
And in that quiet,
he finally heard himself coming home.

It started, as these things often do, with someone telling me I seemed better. There was a time when I thought I'd finished healing. "You're doing so well now," they said — like it was a compliment, like it was a ribbon they could pin to my chest.

I even said it out loud once, not because I believed it, but because I needed it to be true. I needed the story to have an ending — something I could hand to people like proof. A certificate of completion. And for a second, I believed it. That maybe the performance had ended. That maybe I'd walked far enough from the wreckage to start calling it a distant memory.

I smiled. I nodded. I even let the warmth of it wash over me. Look — I made it out. I'm healed. You can stop worrying now. It felt good, for a moment. Maybe even powerful. But later, alone, I couldn't sleep. Because something in me knew I hadn't healed — I had only hidden the wound well enough to be congratulated for surviving it.

Closure. What a strange invention. We sell it like a milestone. Frame it in photos. Write quotes about it. Even tell others to chase it, as if it were a finish line instead of a mirage. I chased it too. I told myself the grief had passed. I told myself I'd forgiven them. I told myself I'd forgiven me. Like it didn't still send shivers through me in the middle of an otherwise normal Tuesday. I packaged the pain into a polite language. "That was a hard time," I'd say, like it hadn't nearly drowned me.

But there's no expiration date on memory. No natural death for a version of you that didn't get to finish its sentence. I still feel him. The one who never got closure. Because closure — real closure — doesn't feel like victory. It feels like absence. It doesn't declare itself. It just stops answering. And even then, sometimes, it still watches from the hallway.

He doesn't scream anymore — he lingers. He flickers. Like a light left on in an empty room, as if he's not sure I'll remember how to get back.

There's a violence in pretending it's over when it's not. Because when people start praising your strength, it gets harder to admit when you're in pain again. You don't want to let them down. You don't want to be the broken record. I wanted to believe I was past it all. You learn to fake peace. You become fluent in "I'm fine." You bury parts of yourself just deep enough that no one trips over them.

But I kept catching glimpses. Not in flashbacks or dreams but in the hesitation before joy. In the way my laughter would land too late. In the echo of a version of me I couldn't quite shut the door on.

That's when I learned something no one tells you about healing: You don't bury the past. You house it. You build a life around it and try not to let it redecorate the walls.

And yet the body remembers. A smell. A song. A silence too long. And suddenly the wound reopens. Not like a fresh cut, but like something that never fully closed in the first place.

There are versions of me still pacing in those rooms. Not angry. Not broken. Just... unwilling to leave. And I don't blame them. I never gave them a proper ending. I gave them applause, a smile, a closing line, but not the silence they deserved.

Some ghosts don't want revenge. They just want you to admit they mattered.

We're taught to look for endings — but some stories refuse. They stretch across years, disguising themselves as growth, hiding in new relationships, echoing through our children. They don't want revenge — just recognition. Not erasure — just space.

I used to be ashamed of how long it was taking. Now I know healing isn't a timeline. It's a terrain. And I'm still crossing mine. Some days on foot, some days crawling, some days just... standing still, listening to the wind for old voices.

I don't owe anyone a conclusion. The past doesn't need me to conquer it. It just wants me to stop pretending I never lived there. I've stopped trying to end the story where it sounds best. Now, I let it echo where it needs to. I let it breathe. I let it stay.

So no, I'm not done. I'm not past all of it. But I'm no longer ashamed of that. I am being honest. And if that's not closure — maybe it's something better.

PART IX
THE ONE WHO WALKED OUT OF THE FIRE

DVOM

He is not a version anymore.
He is the sum of all of them.
The echo, the fire, the author,
and what still remains unwritten.

I thought the end would be louder. I thought when the final version of me collapsed, it would leave smoke and bone, some kind of cinematic finale — scorched earth, cracked mirror, ash in my teeth.

But it wasn't like that. It was quieter. Slower. Almost imperceptible. Like a door left open one day... and never closed again.

There wasn't a line between the man who broke and the man who survived. Just… time. And weather. And a few thousand private moments I never told anyone about. The kind that aren't worthy of memoir but changed everything. The kind where I wasn't heroic or even coherent, I was just still here. Just breathing through it.

I used to write to explain myself. Now I write to *free* myself. And there's a difference. Because this story, these letters, these ghosts, these posthumous fragments of all the men I buried, they were never about proving anything. They were about making space. About letting the versions of me who didn't get closure have their say. Not to bring them back. Just to lay them down gently. With names. With language. With mercy.

I didn't always treat them kindly. Some, I ridiculed. Some, I exiled. Some, I clung to until they suffocated. But in the end, I gave them all the same thing: a voice. And when I stopped needing them to perform, they stopped haunting me.

That's how I know I'm not the same man anymore. Not because I'm healed. Not because I'm better. But because I no longer need to be seen as *undefeated*.

This version of me isn't the strongest. He's not the wisest. He's not the most inspiring. But he's **free.** And I'll take that over applause.

Because after all this time, after the letters and illusions and echoes and dead versions, I finally understand that surviving wasn't the ending. It was the invitation.

So if you're still looking for a climax, a resolution, a final exhale…in a healing poetic way, here it is:

The fire didn't destroy me.
It revealed me.
And this time, I walked out of it.
Not to prove that I could,
but because I no longer needed to burn just to feel real.
I lived, and I kept going.
And I didn't make it out unchanged.
But I made it.

Maybe that's all the closure there ever was.

"Did you think this was the end?
We haven't even met all of us yet,
but there is plenty of good stuff coming up."
~ DVOM ~

CHAPTER X
SELF INFLICTED BIPOLAR

"At some point, I stopped writing versions of myself. And just started living inside them."

This is what came after.

I wrote about the versions of me that died. And then, without ceremony or soundtrack, I accidentally became one of them. It didn't come with collapse or crisis. Just me, hunched over my laptop at 2:07am, arguing with a fictional version of myself I created six drafts ago. Therapists would call it a breakthrough. I call it Tuesday.

See, I wasn't just writing characters, I was emotionally cosplaying them. The Sad One. The Stoic One. The Ghost With Good Lighting. Each one got their monologue, their metaphor, their exit wound. And just when I thought I'd written the last of them, another would crawl out of the wreckage and whisper, "Hey, quick question... what about me?" And of course, I'd write him too. Because I'm generous like that. And, possibly, a little unhinged.

You don't realise you're possessed until you try to do normal things like return a text, cook dinner, scroll mindlessly, and find yourself narrating the rejection of a message as an emotionally informed micro-essay on abandonment, masculinity, and spiritual detachment. "I'm not ghosting her," I told myself. "I'm exploring the silence between unmet needs."

That's when I knew: I was no longer healing. I was publishing my breakdown. But it was polished and resonant. And let's be honest it got engagement. Pain makes a great hook. And boy, was I hooked. On the rhythm. On the reverence. On the intoxicating sense of purpose that comes from narrating your own psychological unravelling like it's an HBO miniseries.

Was it sustainable? Absolutely not. Did I keep going anyway? You're holding the evidence.

Self-inflicted bipolar isn't a diagnosis. It's what happens when you become too good at your own metaphor. When you start bottling sadness and selling it like fragrance.

"This one's called Regret, with top notes of abandonment." "This one's Shame but make it cinematic." "This one's Father Wound—Limited Edition."

They say not to bottle things up. So, I didn't. I decanted every goddamn feeling into prose and poured it into strangers. And then they clapped. Which, somehow, made it worse.

Because once the applause starts, you don't stop the show. Even when you're bleeding backstage. Even when you forget which role is real. Even when you find yourself in the freezer aisle at Woollies arguing with a bag of frozen peas because it reminded you of emotional repression. (I was tired.)

But here's the punchline nobody gets I wasn't pretending. That's what made it believable. I was actually that sad, that layered, that deeply f****d. I just happened to be good at formatting.

And now? I'm suspicious of every emotion I have. Is this a feeling or is it... content?

I try to cry and wonder if the lighting's right. I start journaling and instinctively format the paragraph for carousel slides. I have a breakdown and reach for a caption.

I don't need therapy. I need to be left alone for one goddamn minute without someone asking what font I used for my grief.

There was a time I genuinely thought I was finished with all this. I closed the laptop. I took a walk. I even tried a few of those healthy distractions that Instagram recommends for when you're "*processing heavy emotions*." Five minutes into that walk, I saw a dead crow on the footpath and whispered, "*Same*."

That's when I realised, I wasn't out of the woods. I was the woods. Symbolic, overgrown, and full of unsettling metaphors.

And still—people loved it. They didn't see the spiral. They saw potential.

"She's got anxiety. He's emotionally detached. Let's collab."

Every version of me became a mood board. A caption. A candle scent. A carousel series with a matching font pack.

There were moments—usually at night, sometimes around the third espresso or the seventh deleted message—where I'd pause and ask myself: Am I healing? Or just high-functioning emotional taxidermy?

Because I kept writing about versions that didn't survive while quietly wondering if I was still one of them. And yet, somehow, through it all, I still knew how to sound profound. That's the thing about pain—give it rhythm, and people will mistake it for wisdom.

Even when it's just you sobbing in the pantry because the jar wouldn't open and you think, "Of course. Even my food is emotionally unavailable." There's a poetic injustice in that. It's hilarious. Until it's not.

Until you realise you've designed your entire personality around being heartbreak with eyebrows.

At first, it's empowering. You're the survivor. The artist. The voice of the voiceless. But eventually, it gets weird. You start referring to your own pain like a co-star.

"She was great in Act Two. Really carried the arc."

Friends would tell me, *"This is your best work."* And I'd nod like a creative professional while internally thinking, "I wrote that on the floor. In socks. Crying. Eating cold pasta straight from the container."

There were days I'd wake up and hope I didn't feel anything. I had too much to do. And then, some emotion would arrive—quiet, devastating, dressed like a thought—and I'd sigh, "Alright, but just one paragraph."

That's how it starts. That's how the fracture widens. You dip your toes in the trauma pool for creative effect, and next thing you're backstroking through existential dread with a caption already forming in your head.

And here's the twist—the real clarity came not with triumph, but with boredom. Not a grand epiphany. Just this one dry, quiet truth:

I wanted to be broken. Because brokenness was interesting. It excused the failure. It explained the distance. It justified the attention.

Being whole? That terrified me. Because then I'd have no excuse. No persona. No poetic branding strategy. I'd just be me.

Unfiltered. Boring. Healed.

And who the hell was I without a metaphor?

The thing no one tells you about clarity is that it doesn't arrive like a holy beam of light. It usually shows up at 1:43am when you're half-naked, holding a dirty spoon, crying because you just found a voice memo labelled "Note to Self – Don't Become This Again."

And you did. You became it. All of it. The buzzword. The burnout. The poetic mess in a soft filter. You made yourself a genre.

And somewhere between the captions and the catharsis, you forgot that the goal wasn't to survive beautifully. It was just to survive.

But you couldn't help yourself. You romanticised your own collapse. You made grief marketable. You sold pain like it was merch. And worst of all—you were good at it.

There's a moment I won't forget. I caught my reflection while writing a line about heartbreak and genuinely thought, "Damn. This would make a great promotional reel."

And that's when I knew.

Not that I was broken. Not that I was lost. But that I was performing healing in a costume made of all the versions I had buried.

And it fit perfectly.

That's when the first version of me—the real one, the writer—tried to stage an intervention. He showed up in the back of my mind like a disapproving older brother with a clipboard and a face that said, *"You're exhausting."*

He didn't shout. He didn't cry. He just asked one question:

"So... are you ever going to stop writing the collapse long enough to actually recover from it?"

Rude! But fair. Because recovery isn't poetic. It's brushing your teeth before noon. It's sending the text. Eating the damn salad. It's deciding not to narrate your own emptiness like you're auditioning for the role of "Tragic But Deep Male Lead #1."

Recovery is inconvenient. Unscripted. Unphotogenic. And honestly, I don't know if I'm ready for that.

I've been living in this haunted house of self-mythology for so long, I've started thinking the ghosts pay rent. I know I should move out. Renovate. Rebuild. But part of me still likes the echo. Still likes the drama. Still likes that somewhere, someone will read this and whisper, "God... same."

And that's the final trap, isn't it? Not pain. Not fame. Not even the breakdown.

Relatability.

It's crack for the broken. And I've been mainlining it through every sentence.

But I'm tired now. Not destroyed. Not tragic. Just... tired.

Tired of being a brand. Tired of playing every role. Tired of writing versions of myself just to avoid the terrifying risk of being me—unformatted, unfinished, unfollowed.

So maybe this chapter isn't a cry for help. Maybe it's the punchline. The badly timed joke at the funeral. The whisper after the explosion.

Maybe this is what came after the fire. Not silence. Not peace. Just the weird, beautiful absurdity of still being here.

Still writing. Still wondering if this will get more likes than the one where I cried in the car.

First there was fire. Then ash, then silence, then a whisper that sounded like me. This is what came after.

EXPANSION I
FIELD GUIDE TO THE GHOSTS
Identification, Habits, and Hauntings of Versions That Never Left

"Not every ghost is here to haunt you. Some just want to be remembered."

You don't meet the ghosts all at once. They arrive in fragments. A flicker in the mirror. A delayed reaction to a harmless question. A song you didn't know still had claws.

They don't knock. They don't ask permission. They don't care that you're "doing better now." And the worst part is they don't look like ghosts. They look like you. Just slightly off. A version with tired eyes. A different tone of voice. A hesitation where you used to be sure.

I used to think ghosts were dead people. But the older I got, the more I realised, they're just dead **versions**.

Versions I buried too quickly. Versions I branded too beautifully. Versions I left behind in stories and songs and apartments and arguments that I swore I had healed from.

But they're still here. Not haunting me, haunting **through** me. And this is their guide.

1. The One Who Made Silence a Survival Skill

He doesn't say much. But you'll feel him in your throat. Especially when you're trying to explain how you really feel and the sentence just... dies.

He was born in rooms where you weren't allowed to cry, raised on the belief that composure meant strength. He doesn't trust words. They've betrayed him before. So instead, he flinches. He shuts down. He stares blankly and waits for the conversation to end.

People call him "calm." What they don't see is how loud it is in his head— every emotion rehearsed a hundred times and still considered too risky to share.

You'll often find him lingering after conflict, rewriting what you *should* have said. He won't haunt others. Just you.

2. The Ghost That Confused Suffering With Depth

This one is dramatic. Not in volume, but in gravity. He carries pain like a passport, like proof he's been somewhere you haven't.

He believes he was chosen to suffer. That sadness made him noble. That joy is shallow unless it has trauma underneath. He writes beautifully. He cries silently. And he secretly resents anyone who heals too easily. You'll hear him anytime you laugh too freely. He'll whisper, "You haven't earned this." He'll confuse enlightenment with emotional exhaustion. He's not cruel. But he doesn't want you to move on. Because if you do, what does that say about everything he endured? He prefers grayscale. Hope makes him flinch.

3. The One Who Learned to Perform Healing

This ghost knows his lines. He smiles at the right times. He has an answer ready before the question is even finished. He isn't healed. He's just *prepared*. Prepared to look the part. Prepared to say, "I'm good now," even when the scab hasn't formed.

He thrives in curated spaces. He gets applause for vulnerability. But he never actually rests because real rest requires surrender. And he can't risk not being useful. Not being seen. Not being *liked.*

This one will often show up right before a breakthrough. He'll make you presentable. Digestible. Just broken enough to be interesting, but never so real that someone walks away.

4. The One Who Believed He Had to Earn Love

He works hard. At everything. At being good. At being gentle. At being okay even when he's not. This ghost doesn't haunt like the others. He helps. He fixes. He shows up even when he's empty.

He learned early that love was conditional. So, he became exceptional. Useful. Selfless. Forgivable. He's the reason you apologise when you're the one hurting. He's the voice that says, "Don't make it about you," right as your heart cracks open.

He doesn't want attention. Just approval. He wants to be chosen, but only if he earns it. And that's why he still lingers. He hasn't realised he doesn't need to audition anymore.

5. The One Who Disappears When Things Get Good

You won't always notice him right away. Because he doesn't arrive—he leaves. Just when you start to feel safe. Just when you start to feel seen he panics at peace. He mistakes calm for danger. Joy feels like bait.

He laughs at jokes but doesn't stay for dessert. He writes back a week later. He tells himself he's just tired, but really? He's terrified. Terrified of being known. Terrified that if someone loves him whole, they'll eventually notice the cracks. So, he vanishes first. He always vanishes first.

These are just five. There are more. Some I haven't met yet. Some only show up in mirrors or recordings or the silence right before I fall asleep. But I don't try to fight them anymore. I've stopped asking them to leave. They built this house with bare hands, and with blood, and fear, and poetry, and a thousand whispered apologies. I don't owe them exile. I owe them recognition.

So here it is. Their names. Their patterns. Their echo. Call it haunting. Call it healing. Call it what happens when survival forgets to let go. But whatever you call it, just know: If you've ever felt yourself disappear in the middle of a moment you should have been able to enjoy then it wasn't you. It was one of them. And they are very, very good at making you think they're gone.

EXPANSION II
A LETTER TO THE GHOST WHO WAS NEVER WRITTEN
The One Not Poetic Enough to Be Seen

"He didn't want to be written. He just didn't want to be erased."

I don't know your name. Maybe you never had one. Maybe I never gave you one—not because you didn't deserve it, but because naming you would have meant admitting you existed.

And I wasn't ready for that.

You were the version I didn't put in poems. The one who didn't look good in metaphor. There was nothing cinematic about you. No arc. No glow-up. No redemption. Just ache. Still. Unmarketable. Unresolved.

I didn't write you because I didn't want anyone to see you. Not even me. You were the quiet one. The soft one. The one who held the weight when I was busy performing survival.

And even now, writing this feels like a betrayal. Because you didn't ask for attention. You asked to be left alone. But I think that was just me talking through you— because I didn't know how to face the fact that not all versions get applauded. Some just exist. And hurt. And fade.

You weren't poetic. You were practical. You still went to work. You still smiled at the barista. You still called your parents back. But inside? You were folding in on yourself like paper too wet to hold its shape.

I remember the way you laughed at things just a little too fast, as if joy was a landmine you were trying to skip across. I remember the way you showed up to conversations already halfway gone. The way you'd nod along while your mind played a different scene entirely.

You weren't dramatic. You weren't dangerous. You were just… tired. But not the kind of tired that gets sympathy. The kind that makes people look away. And I did too. I looked away. Because I didn't know what to do with you. You didn't inspire. You didn't fight. You didn't write. You just existed quietly, in the background of better stories.

But now I realise you were the cost of the voice, the captions and the man who lived to tell it. You were the one holding the silence so I could make it sound profound.

And I left you behind. Not with cruelty. With neglect. And that might be worse.

So, this is your letter. Your page. Your proof. That even if I never said it out loud before, you were real.

And I see you now. Not in memory. But in habit. In the way I still downplay joy. In the way I still check the exits when someone gets too close. In the way I still flinch at kindness. You didn't want to be written. But maybe you needed to be witnessed. And I'm sorry it took me this long. But here it is: You're ending. Not with applause, but with presence.

I remember you now. Not as a ghost. But as the man I never let speak. You deserved better. You still do. And this time, I'm not turning the page until you finish your sentence.

EXPANSION III
THE VERSION WHO REFUSED TO PERFORM

Character Study of One's Comfort to Stay Quiet and Invisible.

"Some stories don't need to be told. They just need to be left alone."

He didn't make it into the early drafts. Not because he was irrelevant, but because he wouldn't play along. He didn't want to be poetic. He didn't want to be understood. He didn't even want to be healed.

He wanted to be *left alone.* And you can't build a brand on that. While the other versions wrote captions about survival, delivered metaphors like confessions, this one crossed his arms in the corner and said, "You do realise this is all bullshit, right?"

He didn't like the applause. Didn't trust the sympathy. Refused to be formatted, edited, or redeemed.

You couldn't sell him. Couldn't polish him. Couldn't even explain him. Because he wasn't interested in performance, only protest.

This was the version who rolled his eyes while I turned grief into structure. Who scoffed every time someone called me brave. Who muttered "fuck off" under his breath when I tried to spin pain into a pretty sentence.

He didn't need to be relatable. He needed to be real. And the truth is—I ignored him. For years. Because he didn't help the narrative. He wasn't cinematic. He didn't bleed photogenically. He was angry. Silent. Flatline.

But now I see it. He was the last version who didn't need an audience. Didn't need recognition. Didn't need to be witnessed to feel alive.

He just wanted to exist without being turned into something meaningful.

And I hated him for that. Because deep down, I envied his indifference. His refusal to participate. His absolute rejection of becoming a product.

While I danced through heartbreak for content, he sat still. Unchanged. Unimpressed.

He never asked to be written. But he mattered. Not because he told a story. But because he refused to be one.

Maybe he was the only honest version. The one who wouldn't sell his sadness. The one who wouldn't rehearse. The one who never called it healing.

Maybe the bravest thing he ever did was *not* try to become anything at all.

And maybe that's why I buried him. Because he didn't flatter me. Didn't follow the arc. Didn't perform. But I remember him now. Not with affection. With respect.

He was the version I couldn't monetize. And maybe that means he was the only one who never lied to me.

EXPANSION IV
METHODS OF DISAPPEARING
The Fragmented Performance of Emotional Escapism

"Disappearing wasn't vanishing. It was being too much and not enough at the same time."

It didn't happen all at once. I didn't wake up one day and decide to vanish. I just kept choosing the smaller reaction. The safer sentence. The quieter exit.

And eventually, I wasn't sure if I was leaving things behind or if I'd just stopped arriving at all.

Disappearing isn't one act. It's a collection of strategies. Some look like coping. Others look like charm. Some even get praised. But all of them are ways to slowly and beautifully, efficiently evaporate.

Here are mine.

1. Silence

Not the spiritual kind. Not peaceful. Not earned. This silence was weaponised. Strategic. Say less. Offer less. Reveal nothing. I told myself it was maturity. But it was fear, dressed as control. If they don't know you, they can't reject you. Right?

I muted myself to stay safe. And then forgot how to speak.

2. Charm

A smile is the perfect place to hide. It makes people think you're fine. Sometimes it even makes you believe it. I got good at reading the room. Knowing what version of myself would be most welcomed. And I served him. Over and over. With flair.

But that's the problem with performance: If you do it well enough, no one ever thinks to ask who's missing.

3. Competence

I became exceptional. At work. At empathy. At anticipating what people needed before they asked. It felt like love. But it was self-erasure.

I stayed useful so no one would notice how lonely I was. I stayed efficient so no one would ask if I needed anything. It worked. Too well.

4. Intellectualising

Feel it? No thanks. Let's write about it. Let's narrate it. Let's build a psychological framework and diagram our triggers.

Turn pain into poetry. Grief into captions. Disassociation into content. Make it look profound, so you don't have to admit you're still bleeding. Make it beautiful so no one realises you haven't actually healed.

5. Distraction

Work. Hustle. Creativity. Even healing itself. I turned them all into projects. Everything became an excuse not to sit still. Stillness was dangerous. Stillness made the ghosts louder.

So I ran. I stayed productive. And I called it progress.

6. Control

I stopped taking emotional risks. No new friends. No big moves. No spontaneous joy. Just manageable doses of existence. I mastered how to keep things steady. And lost the ability to let things surprise me.

I told myself it was wisdom. But really, it was disappearance with a calendar.

All of these methods worked. Until they didn't. Until I looked in the mirror and saw only a collection of responses. Until someone asked, "How are you?" and I realised I didn't have access to an honest answer. Because I hadn't just disappeared from others. I'd disappeared from myself. Not in some tragic, cinematic way. Not in a way that gets you rescued.

Just quietly. Skilfully. Entirely.

And now? Now I'm trying to reappear. But I'm not sure where to start. Because becoming visible again means being seen in the places I once hid. And I'm not sure yet if I'm ready to be that honest.

EXPANSION V
I WAS NEVER THE CHOSEN ONE
Pain Was Special, But It Meant I Was Human

"I didn't need to be chosen. I needed to stop auditioning."

There was a time I believed the pain made me special. Like I'd been given a darker script than everyone else. Like the universe looked at me and said, "Yes, him. Make it hurt more there."

I thought my sadness meant I was chosen. Not lucky. Not blessed. Just *selected* to carry the emotional weight of everyone who never said the quiet parts out loud. And I wore it like a purpose. Like I was doing something noble by breaking publicly. I turned grief into gospel. Wrote captions like commandments. Spoke about my healing like it came with a title.

But the truth? I wasn't chosen. I was just hurting. Just like everyone else. The only difference was—I made it poetic. I dressed it up. I gave it language and rhythm and resonance. And for a while, that was enough to make me feel important. I had followers. I had tone. I had a haunting kind of gravitas. But deep down, I knew. I wasn't different. I wasn't deep. I was just very, very good at framing despair.

I used to look at people who seemed happy— truly, stupidly, obnoxiously at peace— and feel superior. As if their joy was shallow. As if they hadn't earned it. As if happiness was for the untested. But I see it now. That wasn't wisdom. It was envy. Because they didn't need the pain to feel like they mattered. They didn't need tragedy to write. They didn't need to be broken to feel seen.

And me? I built an entire identity on being the one who *got it*. The one who felt too much. The one who saw beneath the surface. Turns out, there is no surface. Turns out, we're all aching. Just some of us do it quietly. I thought I was chosen. But I was just loud. And now I'm learning to be soft. Learning to stop trying to win suffering like it's a prize. Because no one is keeping score.

And even if they were, I don't want the trophy anymore. I'd rather be boring and whole than brilliant and broken. I'd rather write badly and feel okay than write perfectly and want to vanish.

I was never the chosen one. I was just the one who kept writing through it when I probably should have rested. And maybe that's the most honest thing I've ever said.

EXPANSION VI
A LETTER LEFT UNSENT
Closure Deserved A Devastating End

"This wasn't forgiveness. It was restraint."

I won't be poetic. You don't deserve that.

I've rewritten this a hundred times in my head only to not find the right words, but to make sure none of them let you back in. You're not a ghost. Ghosts have grief behind them. You were something else. And still, I almost wrote to you. Not because you earned it. But because part of me thought closure needed a ceremony. A full stop. Something neat.

But this isn't neat. It never was. You left wreckage and waited for applause. You spun silence into guilt and called it peace.

I gave you the most fragile parts of me— the unfinished ones, the uncertain ones— and you held them like you were waiting to drop them just hard enough that I'd blame myself.

And I did. For a long time. But not anymore.

So no, you don't get the letter. You don't get the closure. You don't get to be the final chapter in a story you never stayed long enough to read. This isn't forgiveness. This isn't grace. It's just me, finally realizing that silence can be sacred too.

You'll never read this. And I think that's the point. Not all stories need an audience. Some just need to end.

BONUS CHAPTER
INTERVIEW WITH THE FUTURE SELF

"You're not running out of time. You're running out of versions."

PRESENT SELF: What is this, am I dreaming? No, wait. No. This isn't happening. There shouldn't be voices in my head.

FUTURE SELF: It's not in your head. It's in your timeline.

PRESENT SELF: Okay... no. No. Whatever this is, I didn't ask for.

FUTURE SELF: But you did. You wrote to me. And now I'm writing back.

PRESENT SELF: This can't be real.

FUTURE SELF: It's not...It's necessary.

<pause>

FUTURE SELF: You're late.

PRESENT SELF: Late to what?

FUTURE SELF: This. The moment. The version of you that was supposed to begin.

PRESENT SELF: Is this supposed to be a metaphor, or—

FUTURE SELF: No metaphors. Not this time. You used them to dodge the truth. I speak plainly.

PRESENT SELF: Okay. Then what do you want from me?

FUTURE SELF: I want you to stop pretending this version is sustainable. The one you're performing. The one who wakes up with ghosts and calls it growth. The one who writes letters to me and ignores what I'm trying to say back.

PRESENT SELF: I never ignored you.

FUTURE SELF: No?

"Dear future self, I'm writing from the wreckage of a past life I couldn't save. I've buried so many versions of myself just to make it here. And still... I don't know if I'm enough. But you—you need to believe again. Because you're all we've got left."

You wrote that. Then kept doing everything in your power to become another version to bury.

PRESENT SELF: That was then. I'm trying.

FUTURE SELF: No, you're writing. There's a difference.

PRESENT SELF: What do you think all this is?

FUTURE SELF: A delay tactic. You narrate your healing instead of living it. You publish your reckoning instead of facing it. You perform truth like it's a monologue. I'm not here for your language. I'm here for your alignment.

PRESENT SELF: You think I don't want that?

FUTURE SELF: I think you're scared. Because if you aligned - really aligned - you wouldn't be able to keep any of this. Not the performance. Not the brand. Not the sadness you turned into a safety net.

PRESENT SELF: That sadness kept me alive.

FUTURE SELF: And now it's keeping you *here*. In the middle. In the almost.

PRESENT SELF: I didn't ask to be interrogated.

FUTURE SELF: You did. Every time you wrote to me. Every time you said, "You're all we've got left."

PRESENT SELF: So what now? You've come back to judge me?

FUTURE SELF: No. I came back to *warn* you. Again. Because the last time you didn't listen, we lost a version. One that mattered. One that nearly made it.

PRESENT SELF: How many more warnings do I get?

FUTURE SELF: One.

PRESENT SELF: ...And if I miss it?

FUTURE SELF: Then this conversation becomes memory. Then I become the version who tried. And you become the one we bury next.

PRESENT SELF: That's a hell of a threat.

FUTURE SELF: It's not a threat. It's protocol. Every version that lingers too long in misalignment gets replaced. You know that. You wrote it. I just came to remind you what it sounds like when truth stops whispering and starts giving ultimatums.

PRESENT SELF: So what, you want me to become you?

FUTURE SELF: No. I want you to *choose* to. That's the difference between a dead version and a living one. Intention.

PRESENT SELF: You seem calm for someone who's supposedly me.

FUTURE SELF: That's because I already lived through this part. The pain. The reckoning. The collapse. I let it end. I didn't drag the wreckage into every sentence like a badge. I let it burn.

PRESENT SELF: And then what?

FUTURE SELF: Then I began.

BEGIN

Somewhere, a braver version of you is already inhabiting the life you keep deferring, writing the pages, taking the risks, inhabiting the space you say isn't ready yet. He isn't urging you to sprint after him or make up for lost years; the distance doesn't interest him. What he wants is far simpler: that you take the first unglamorous step today, the one that turns "someday" into motion. Begin, and the gap between you will start to close on its own.

FINAL CHAPTER
THE ONE WHO LISTENED

"I wasn't silent. I was listening. You just weren't quiet enough to hear me."

You don't know me. But I know you. I was there…. for all of it. I watched the others speak. Perform. Beg. Collapse. Rise. I stayed quiet. Not because I had nothing to say. But because I knew no one was listening.

I was the one who stayed behind when you left the room. The one who held the silence when the chapter ended. The one who waited between your sentences, wondering if you'd ever stop writing long enough to actually feels anything.

You didn't see me. But I saw you. I watched you rewrite grief until it made sense. Watched you dress the wreckage in metaphors. Watched you bury version after version and then call it *healing*. I didn't intervene. I wasn't sent to save you. I was sent to witness.

Every time you almost broke but decided instead to turn the pain into art, I saw it. Every time someone praised your vulnerability without knowing what it cost, I heard the silence that followed. And when the noise got too loud, the captions, the followers, the clever prose, the polished heartbreak…I waited. Because I knew. Eventually, you'd run out of voices. Eventually, everyone who wanted to be heard would speak. Everyone who wanted closure would get their chapter and you'd be left with the only thing you couldn't explain away:

Me.

The part of you that never needed to be profound. The part that doesn't perform. The one who remembers *everything*. The day you stopped narrating, I woke up. Not to shout. Not to rescue you. Just to speak. Because it got quiet. And for the first time, I wasn't the only one listening. You made it loud for so long so no one would hear what the quiet was trying to say.

But silence doesn't forget. It waits. And now, so do I. You don't have to write me a chapter. You must let me stay.

Elliott Collinson

I didn't write this book to be understood.
I wrote it because silence stopped working.
Every version I buried,
left something behind worth saving.

AFTERWORD

ACKNOWLEDGEMENTS
(The Sentimental Ghost)

There were times I didn't think this book would make it — not because the words wouldn't come, but because too many of them already had. They came when I was tired. When I was avoiding. When I was unravelling. And each time, I'd think: Surely that's enough now. But the truth is, I wasn't writing a book. I was writing a funeral. A eulogy for every version of me that didn't survive the performance. Every self I tried on. Every one of them I quietly fired when the applause stopped.

So, if this book is anything, it's not an achievement. It's a reckoning. And if it somehow helped you feel less alone, then maybe some part of me still matters.

There are people who helped me hold this together - even when I wasn't sure what "this" was.

My parents, Terry & Maxine: the incredible souls and original architects: Everything I became. The stubbornness, the emotional curiosity, the need to build something out of nothing, started with you. You didn't raise a writer. You raised a question that kept needing answers.

You never flinched when I veered into madness. You never asked me to be less. I am, quite literally, built from your belief. An individual that strives for achievement, yes — but also for meaning. For something real. For something that might one day be worthy of the sacrifices you made.

You gave me the room to become difficult, and the patience to survive it. You taught me that strength doesn't always roar, sometimes it's just showing up. And even when I disappeared into the obsession of becoming, I always knew you were still there, holding space for the version of me I hadn't yet met.

I owe you more than thanks. I owe you the man I became when everything else fell away.

Gina. You're not a literary agent but you might as well be one. You're something much more dangerous. A force. A mentor. A conspirator. A quietly explosive guide through the beautiful wreckage of this industry. You didn't just back me — you bet on me, even when I was hedging my own story. Thank you for calling bullshit when it needed to be called and for reminding me that craft without conviction is just a hobby.

To the artists and strangers who don't know they saved me: You showed me what it looked like to bleed on your own terms. I watched you break in public, rebuild in silence, and speak with a voice that hadn't been trained to be liked. Some of you will never read this. Some of you are woven between the lines. Either way, you're in here.

To the ghosts: No one tells you how hard it is to outlive your own performances. You should've seen some of you — charismatic, tragic, poetic, absolutely exhausting. But you got me here. You dragged me through delusion and denial and desperation until I had no choice but to sit down and write something real. You were terrible at long-term planning, but god you made great content.

And to the reader: If you made it this far, I suspect you've buried a few versions of yourself, too. Maybe you performed for too long. Maybe you got tired of being the strong one. Maybe you're not sure who you are without the pain. If that's you, just know this: You're not broken. You're just becoming someone new. It's messy. It's slow. It's not very Instagrammable. But it's real.

Lastly, to the version of me who thought this book needed to be perfect: Relax. It's done now. The ghosts have been fed. The metaphors have been milked. You can go outside. And no, no one's giving you a ribbon.

ABOUT THE AUTHOR

Elliott Collinson is a writer, producer, and former athlete (of no notable history) who believes in going too far, then writing his way back. He doesn't claim to be a literary voice in the traditional sense, but he does claim the wreckage of his very colourful past. His work comes from a place most people spend their lives trying to avoid: the deep end of self-invention.

Born in Perth and now based in Sydney, Elliott's path to authorship wasn't linear. He didn't find writing through academia or quiet reflection; he found it by losing himself inside characters he never intended to live through. What began as screenwriting became a kind of emotional possession. He calls it method writing, a creative process so immersive it blurred the boundary between fiction and identity. The result was something he now refers to as self-inflicted bipolar storytelling - the psychological whiplash of embodying too many truths at once without ever stepping back.

Dead Versions of Me is his first book, part memoir, part emotional autopsy, and part literary graveyard. It's a reckoning with the selves we become while chasing meaning, survival, applause, or silence. Through poetic narrative and psychological grit, Elliott offers not healing, but honesty. And sometimes, that's the more dangerous thing.

He is currently developing multiple companion projects across graphic novels, screen adaptations, and experimental formats through Dead Versions Creative. His diary is full. His ghosts are louder than ever. And somehow, he's just getting started.

SOCIALS

Instagram: *@deadversionsofme*

Website: *www.deadversionsofme.com*

Dead Versions Of Me

Elliott Collinson

www.ingramcontent.com/pod-product-compliance
Lightning Source LLC
Chambersburg PA
CBHW042319090526
44583CB00025BA/3141